The Century

for Young People

For a complete overview of the most eventful
hundred years in human history, you'll want to read these
companion volumes:

The Century for Young People:
Becoming Modern America: 1901–1936

The Century for Young People:
Defining America: 1936–1961

PETER JENNINGS
TODD BREWSTER

Adapted by Jennifer Armstrong

TheCentury
for Young People

Changing America
1961–1999

DELACORTE PRESS

Text copyright © 1999 by ABC, Inc.
New introduction copyright © 2009 by Brewster, Inc.

This is the third volume of a three-volume adaptation of *The Century for
Young People,* by Peter Jennings and Todd Brewster. Based upon the work
The Century, by Peter Jennings and Todd Brewster, published by Doubleday
Books, a division of Random House, Inc., New York, in 1998.

Visit us on the Web! www.randomhouse.com/teens

Educators and librarians, for a variety of teaching tools, visit us at
www.randomhouse.com/teachers

Library of Congress Cataloging-in-Publication Data
Armstrong, Jennifer.
The century for young people / Peter Jennings, Todd Brewster ; adapted
by Jennifer Armstrong. — 1st trade pbk. ed.
p. cm.
Includes index.
ISBN 978-0-385-73769-2 (v. 1 : trade pbk.) — ISBN 978-0-385-90682-1
(v. 1 : glb) — ISBN 978-0-375-89397-1 (e-book) 1. History, Modern—20th
century—Juvenile literature. 2. History, Modern—20th century—Pictorial
works. I. Jennings, Peter, 1938–2005. Century. II. Brewster, Todd. Century.
III. Title.
D422.A76 2009
909.82—dc22
2009008437

The text of this book is set in 12-point Sabon.
Printed in the United States of America
10 9 8 7 6 5 4 3 2 1
First Trade Paperback Edition

For our children:
Elizabeth, Christopher, and Jack

CONTENTS

INTRODUCTION

If you are one of those people who consider history to be the study of dry and boring facts, please think again. You are in for a surprise when you read these books. Well-told history is as compelling as any great novel or movie. It is full of drama, tension, interesting characters, and fantastic events. That is what you will find here, in this, the history—or should we simply say "story"?—of the twentieth century.

One hundred years may seem like a long time ago, but actually, this is fairly recent history. It is really not too far removed from your life today—and the story of the twentieth century is not just any old story. It is the story of your parents and grandparents, of the world they were born into and the one they helped create. And while some of the events described here happened in faraway places decades ago, you will probably recognize that some things are the way they are now because of what happened then. In other words, this is not only your parents' and grandparents' story; it is your story, too.

One of the most important reasons to study history is to help us understand the present. Think of how old you are today. Now think about your parent or grandparent or even great-grandparent at your age. Without so much as blinking, you can list five things that did not exist in their lifetime. At the beginning of the twentieth century, there was no automobile, no television, no radio, and certainly no Internet. African Americans in the South lived in segregated communities; few women worked outside the home, and none had the right to vote. So how did we get here from there?

Consider global affairs. When your parents and grandparents were growing up, America's biggest enemy was the Soviet Union, which included modern-day Russia and neighboring countries. From the end of World War II in 1945 until 1991, when the Soviet Union collapsed under its own weight, America and the Soviet Union often stood nose to nose. In what we now refer to as the Cold War, a nuclear confrontation between the two countries was a persistent threat, though thankfully, one that was never realized.

Today, the Soviet Union is long gone, replaced, in one sense, by America's twenty-first-century enemy: radical factions of the religion of Islam. Yet you will be interested to read about the events of 1979, when rebels inspired by the Ayatollah Ruhollah Khomeini, the long-exiled spiritual leader of Iranian Shiite

Muslims, challenged what he called the decadent West by overthrowing the American-backed Shah of Iran and installing an anti-American regime. Looking back, we can now say that when Khomeini's followers seized the American embassy in Tehran and held 52 people hostage for 444 days, they gave us a hint of what was to come twenty-some years later: the events of September 11, 2001, the wars in Iraq and Afghanistan, and the threat of Islamic terrorism that you live with today. If you were a small child on September 11, 2001 (or not yet born), that date may seem like just another landmark in our history. But for many others, it is the defining moment of the twenty-first century, *their* twenty-first century. These books will help you understand this and other world-shattering events that shaped our lives.

Another way to think of history is to say that it is the study of change. Consider this: the adolescents of the early 1900s were not referred to as teenagers—the word wasn't even used until 1941—and as late as 1920, children were unlikely to finish, and often even to start, high school. Teens were needed to work the farms in what was still largely an agricultural society. Certainly no one would have imagined that there could be such a thing as a distinct teen culture. The rise of popular music, which came with the phonograph and then the radio, made such a culture possible. So did urbanization, industrialization, and prosperity, which by the 1950s gave families the luxury to let young people stay in school longer, maybe even go to college, and to be "teenagers."

Technology has always been among the biggest agents of change, and as the story of the twentieth century shows, it can introduce itself unexpectedly. When Henry Ford built the first affordable cars in the United States, he imagined that he was creating a machine that would enhance rural life. The first Model Ts had the potential to double as farm tractors. But in the end the automobile had the opposite effect: once people could get into their Fords and travel, they could see worlds that had long been beyond them, and so a kind of new mobility entered American life, with children growing up and moving far away to pursue lives wholly different from those of their parents. Similarly, the first computers— room-sized behemoths created in the late 1940s— were designed almost exclusively as tools for the scientific community, not as the research, communication, and entertainment platforms we consider them today. It was not until the early 1980s that most people had computers in their offices and homes.

The technological, intellectual, and commercial explosions that greeted the twentieth century made many people dream of a day when a permanent harmony would descend over the globe, but sadly, that was not to be. In fact, if there was one common teenage experience the world over, it was that most ancient of human activities, war. Beginning in 1914, large armies in Europe engaged in horrific battle. People called that first global conflict the Great War, thinking that it would be the last such battle in human history. Now we call it World War I, followed as it was by World War II, just twenty years later, and by the persistent late-twentieth-century (and now early-twenty-first-century) fears that we were (or are) on the brink of World War III.

More than nine million people, much of Europe's youth, died in the Great War alone. But as you contemplate such numbing numbers, it may be more powerful to think not just about how many lives were lost, but also about whose lives were lost. If there had been no war in 1914, maybe one of those who died would have grown up to be a scientist who discovered a cure for cancer or a humanitarian who solved the world's hunger problem. Maybe Germans, absent the humiliation of defeat, would never have listened to the perverse racist message of Adolf Hitler, who led that country into the nightmare that could be stopped only by an even greater war that killed even more people. Many historians are now convinced that had there been no World War I, there would likely have been no World War II and no Cold War, for each, it seems, led inevitably to the next.

With all its wars and devastation, the twentieth century may seem like a bleak episode, a sad study. But as you continue your journey through these three volumes, hold that thought. Loud and sensational events always mask slower, deeper trends, and in the twentieth century the more gradual and less sensational changes mark a time of glorious achievement.

Because the forces of liberty did win that protracted battle between East and West, there are more people living in free and democratic societies today than at any time in human history. In our own country, freedom was extended to millions who had long been denied it by persistent traditions of racial, gender, and ethnic discrimination. Only after defeating Hitler were the American armed forces, in 1948, desegregated.

Science produced new weapons of frightening magnitude in the twentieth century, but it also found ways to erase disease and prolong life. Perhaps the century's most significant change is represented by this fact: if you had been born in 1905, you could expect to live only forty-nine years. By contrast, babies born in America today, as you read this, will likely live to seventy-eight, and some— many, in fact—will live to see the twenty-second century.

In a century when it sometimes seemed that some life-changing innovation was being introduced every week, there were also many remarkable acts of human will by people who, stuck in situations that seemed utterly hopeless, found the courage to ask "why?" The twentieth century produced so many more heroes than villains, people like Thomas Edison and Bill Gates, Jackie Robinson and Rosa Parks, George Marshall and Martin Luther King Jr., and it no doubt produced many more who never became famous, who moved quietly, even silently, behind the drama to make life better. They pushed for justice and beauty and good and not only asked "why?" but, thinking of how things could be made better, also asked "why not?" I hope all of you reading this book will emerge inspired by their example. As my colleague Peter Jennings used to write when signing the original edition of *The Century for Young People*, "The next century is yours." To that, I would add a challenge: "Make your mark on it."

—Todd Brewster

CHAPTER 1

Into the Streets

1961–1969

The 1960s were a turning point in America's history. Ideas that had been introduced in the 1950s now began to gain momentum. The civil rights movement, begun as a series of peaceful protests, grew more violent as some of its followers became impatient with the slow pace of change. U.S. involvement in the war in Southeast Asia, intended to hold back the tide of Communism, grew rapidly. And the new political awareness of youth bloomed almost overnight into a rejection of many of the values of an older generation. Both exciting and confusing, full of hope and despair, the 1960s witnessed a cascade of events that changed the way Americans looked at themselves, at each other, and at the rest of the world.

1

At first America's youth eagerly answered the call to service by President John F. Kennedy. As a result of the baby boom, there were now more young people in college than there were farmers in the United States. The youthful president was the natural leader of this army of students, and one of the first missions he created for them was the Peace Corps.

The Peace Corps was a generous way of extending American influence into parts of the world where poverty and ignorance could make the promises of Communism appealing. Young, enthusiastic volunteers were sent to underdeveloped countries to build schools, teach modern agricultural practices, and develop community services. When Kennedy began the Peace Corps just three months into his presidency, hundreds, then thousands of college students jumped at the chance to serve.

Marnie Muller, who was born in 1942, was one of the willing volunteers in the early years of the Peace Corps.

When Kennedy was elected there was definitely a feeling that he was going to somehow lead the country in a different way. He was young and handsome, and he talked a language that I could understand. When he said, "Ask not what your country can do for you, ask what you can do for your country," it struck a very profound chord in me. I was a junior in college when he announced the formation of the Peace Corps, and I immediately thought, "I'm going to get an application, and I'm going to join this Peace Corps." I was going to go and help the poor people of the world do something better with their lives. The idea was to go there and help people to help themselves.

I was assigned to an extremely poor barrio on the northern side of Guayaqil [a city in Ecuador], on a very picturesque hill, full of cane shacks. The running water only went up to a certain place on the hill. Beyond that, water had to be carried in buckets up to people's houses. Many of the houses had dirt floors, and none of them had windows. There were holes in the roofs. There was garbage and sewage overflowing down the hill. It was a pretty big shock to me. My job was to organize activities for a new community center, which was built by previous volunteers. You have to understand, I was a twenty-one-year-old girl. I not only had to live in a very rough-and-tumble community, but I then had to try and work some miracle within the community. I was alternately thrilled, moved, excited, terrified, and filled with the desire to go home.

We had a library in the community center. We had mechanics classes in there. We organized football teams for the boys to play. Whatever the community wanted, we developed. Out of that grew more serious projects such as a preschool. Out of the sewing classes grew an economic development project where the women made mosquito nets and sold them to CARE to make money. On the one hand, I was very accepted in the community. On the other hand, whenever you're a First World person working in the Third World, there is always a certain anger and resentment toward you.

Out of the activities at the center grew a notion that the community could begin to demand bigger, more fundamental changes. And when we began to deal with the true needs of the community, we got into some trouble. One of the first indications that something was wrong occurred at a party I threw at my house. The president of the Small Business Organization pulled me aside and pointed to somebody in the room and said, "What is he doing here? He's a Communist." And then sometime after that, when the people in the community marched on the *municipio,* the city government, to demand a new sewage system, the money for the center disappeared. Then the U.S. ambassador called me in and warned me not to enter into the politics of the country.

Many of us suspected that there was

something else going on, that there was another purpose for our being there that we weren't told about. There was something wrong with young, inexperienced kids coming like gangbusters into these Third World communities as though we knew everything about the world—as though we knew how to help these poor people. There was a certain arrogance about our being there, and it was very disturbing for us to find that out.

More and more, the developing world became the battleground for the Cold War between democracy and Communism. The United States and the Soviet Union both tried to extend their influence over smaller, poorer countries around the world. Cuba, an island nation just south of Florida, became Communist when Fidel Castro took power in 1959. Tensions ran high between Cuba and the United States, especially after President Kennedy mounted a secret invasion of the island in 1961. The invasion at the Bay of Pigs was a total failure.

The leader of the Soviet Union, Nikita Khrushchev, sensed from the Bay of Pigs disaster that Kennedy might be weak. He decided to challenge the young president by arming Cuba with nuclear missiles aimed at the United States. The idea of an enemy missile base so close to home terrified Americans. Still, photographs taken from American reconnaissance planes did not show any missiles ready to launch—yet. In an attempt to keep the Soviet missiles from reaching their launch site, President Kennedy ordered a blockade of all Russian ships headed to Cuba. Then he waited to see what the Russians would do.

Sixteen navy destroyers and three cruisers blocked access to Cuba while twenty-five Soviet merchant ships stayed on course for the island. Around the country—around the world—people watched nervously. In a California high school, a student reportedly broke down, sobbing, "I don't want to die." Pope John XXIII pleaded with Kennedy and Khrushchev to consider their moral duty to the world. At last, after thirteen nail-biting days, Khrushchev turned his ships back in exchange for a promise that America would never invade Cuba. The Cuban missile crisis was over, but the feeling endured that the end of the world might be only a heartbeat away.

Crisis followed crisis as the country continued to struggle with the issue of civil rights. The nonviolent campaign of the fifties, led by black churches, had made progress, but for many people it was not enough. More and more African Americans felt bitter toward a white power structure that still denied them basic equality. And many now grew impatient with Martin Luther King Jr. and other moderate leaders. They also began to doubt the support of the federal government. The Supreme Court had ruled again and again that segregation was unconstitutional. Yet so long as local authorities refused to change anything, these legal victories were hollow. Only the federal government could ensure that the local authorities obeyed the law.

In 1961 the Supreme Court ruled that segregated interstate bus terminals were unconstitutional. A group of activists calling themselves Freedom Riders rode buses into southern cities, hoping to be arrested. They wanted to force the federal government to stand up for them and uphold the Constitution. But it seemed that the Freedom Riders were on their own. In one Alabama town a mob set a bus on fire. In Birmingham, Alabama, the Ku Klux Klan attacked a bus with the full support of the police commissioner. In Montgomery, Alabama, home of Rosa Parks, a white mob went after the Freedom Riders with metal pipes and baseball bats, while the city's police chief declared that his department had "no intention of standing guard for a bunch of troublemakers coming into our city." When Martin Luther King showed up in Montgomery the next day to lead a church rally, the church was firebombed. Finally, U.S. marshals arrived to drive the white mob back. Attorney General Robert Kennedy, the president's brother, asked King to observe a cooling-off period. Organizer James Farmer replied to reporters with righteous anger, "Please tell the attorney general that we have been cooling off for three hundred and fifty years."

Diane Nash, born in 1938, was one of the student Freedom Riders who joined the struggle against segregation.

Igrew up on the South Side of Chicago, and while there was segregation there, I didn't really notice it that much. I always knew things were much worse in the South. While I ran into some discrimination growing up, it wasn't until I went to school in Nashville, Tennessee, that I experienced real segregation. When I arrived at Fisk University, I visited a few of the places near campus that were available to blacks, but everything else was segregated. I resented not being able to go downtown to the Woolworth's and have lunch with a friend. Also, when I was downtown, I saw lots of blacks sitting out on the curb or on the ground eating their lunches because they weren't allowed to sit in the restaurants and eat. It was so demeaning. The first time I had to use a women's rest room marked Colored was pretty humiliating, too.

Pretty soon I started looking for an organization—someone, somewhere—that was trying to do something to change segregation. I heard about a series of workshops conducted by Reverend James Lawson, who was extremely well versed in nonviolence. So I went to these workshops, and I listened very carefully. After a few weeks I decided this nonviolence couldn't possibly have any impact. But because they were the only group in Nashville that was trying to make a change, I kept going.

In the fall of 1959 we started going to restaurants downtown and trying to get served. When we were refused service, we would ask to see the manager, ask him why we were being refused service, and then tell him we thought it was morally wrong. We called that testing. In February of 1960 we heard on the radio that sit-ins had begun in other southern cities, and then we decided to have our sit-ins at the same chains that the students were targeting in other cities.

By 1962 I had left Fisk University to devote all my time to the civil rights movement. In May I was in Mississippi, where the bus system was still legally segregated, encouraging black young people to sit at the front of the bus and conducting workshops on nonviolence to prepare students for the things they needed to know in order to join the Freedom Riders. I was twenty-three at the time, and since I was encouraging these minors to do something illegal, a warrant was issued for my arrest, charging me with contributing to the delinquency of minors. I faced a two-and-a-half-year jail term, and I was about six months pregnant with my first child. My husband drove me down to Jackson and I surrendered to the sheriff, and the following Monday I surrendered to the court. I sat in the first bench in the first row and refused to move to the rear when the bailiff ordered me to do so, so I was put in jail for ten days for contempt of court.

Those days were really hard. The jail had so many cockroaches that I soon learned to sleep during the day so that I could sit up at night and dodge them as they dropped off the ceiling onto my cot. One night there was an insect that was so large I could actually hear it walking across the floor. I had taken a toothbrush, comb, and my vitamin pills (since I was expecting), a change of underwear, and an extra skirt and blouse, because I knew I was going to jail. But the prison officials would not let me have anything, not a toothbrush, not toothpaste, nothing. I remember combing my hair with my fingers and working out a way to brush my teeth. I emerged from the experience even stronger because I learned that I could get along with nothing if I had to—except food and water, perhaps.

When you are faced with a situation of injustice or oppression, if you change yourself and become somebody who cannot be oppressed, then the world has to set up against a new you. We students became people who could not be segregated. They could have killed us, but they could not segregate us any longer. Once that happened, the whole country was faced with a new set of decisions. I think most of the students that were participating were confident that we could change the world. I still think we can.

Martin Luther King had not given up hope of a better America. On August 28, 1963, he addressed nearly a quarter of a million demonstrators at the March on Washington, the first massive display of sixties "people power." The people in the audience— many of them the great-grandchildren of slaves— had come together in one of the crowning moments of the civil rights movement. King stood at the Lincoln Memorial, beneath the statue of Abraham Lincoln, and gave one of the most stirring speeches in American history. "I have a dream," he said, describing his vision of America as it could be and as it should be. "When we let freedom ring, when we let it ring from every village and hamlet, from every state and every city, we will be able to speed up that day when all of God's children, black men and white men, Jews and Gentiles, Protestants and Catholics, will all be able to join hands and sing in the words of the old Negro spiritual, 'Free at last! Free at last! Thank God almighty, we are free at last!'"

King's words were electrifying. For the first time,

many white Americans understood that the civil rights workers were patriots, challenging the nation to live up to its best traditions. The March on Washington was a grand, hopeful spectacle. But only two weeks later a bomb exploded in the Sixteenth Street Baptist Church in Birmingham, Alabama, killing four young black girls as they were putting on their choir robes.

On Friday, November 22, 1963, President Kennedy was in Dallas, Texas, trying to smooth his relationship with members of the Democratic Party there. Many white southern Democrats had felt he was too supportive of the civil rights movement, and with an election coming up, JFK wanted to repair his image in the South.

The president and the First Lady, Jackie Kennedy, were in the backseat of an open convertible, waving to the crowds lining the parade route in downtown Dallas. The president smiled and waved, raising his right hand to push back his hair, when he suddenly slumped forward, clutching his throat. Almost immediately his head was thrown back by a second impact. President John Fitzgerald Kennedy had been shot. Secret Service agents flung themselves toward the dying president and his wife, who was unhurt but covered with her husband's blood. John Connally, the governor of Texas, had also been shot, though not fatally.

Reporter Richard Stolley, born in 1928, covered the assassination of the president for *Life* magazine.

On November 22, 1963, one of my colleagues, who was watching the AP [Associated Press] ticker, suddenly shouted to me that Kennedy had been shot in Dallas. I got on the phone to the New York office, and they told me to get to Dallas as fast as I could.

I set up a bureau office in a downtown hotel. At about six o'clock I got a phone call from a *Life* [reporter]. She had heard from a cop that a Dallas businessman [Abraham Zapruder] had been in Dealey Plaza with a movie camera and had photographed the assassination from beginning to end. If that film actually existed, I just knew I had to get it, but I wasn't sure where to look. So I picked up the Dallas phone book and just ran my fingers down the Z's, and God, there it was: Zapruder, comma, Abraham. I called the number every fifteen minutes for about five hours, but no one picked up. Finally, late that evening, around eleven, this weary voice answered, and I said, "Is this Abraham Zapruder?" He said, "Yes." "Is it true that you photographed the assassination?" "Yes." "Have you seen the film?" "Yes." And then I said, "Can I come out and see it now?" And he said, "No. I'm too upset. I'm too tired. Come to my office at nine."

I got there at 8:00 A.M. Saturday. Zapruder was slightly annoyed that I was an hour early, but he let me come in anyway. Inside the room were four very grim-faced Secret Service agents who had also come down to see the film. Zapruder got out this creaky old projector, with, of course, no sound, and he beamed the film up on a plain white wall. Within just a few seconds I knew that I was experiencing the most dramatic moment in my entire career. I was sitting there with these Secret Service agents as they watched a film of their failure at their number one job, which was to protect the president. We watched the motorcade snake around onto Elm Street around Dealey Plaza. It went behind a sign and Kennedy was briefly out of the scene. The next time we saw the president, his hands were up around his throat, and Connally's mouth was open and he was howling in pain—they had both already been shot. Jackie turned her head and looked quizzically at her husband. Less than two or three seconds later, without warning, the whole right side of President Kennedy's head just exploded in pink froth. Everyone watching the film in the room, including the Secret Service agents, just went, "Ugh!" It was like we had been gut-punched. Zapruder, who had already seen the film, turned his head away just before the image of Kennedy getting shot appeared on the screen. It was an absolutely astounding moment. There was Jackie crawling up onto the trunk, and Secret Service agent Clint Hill leaping up onto the car, pushing Jackie back in, and holding on for dear life as the limo sped away to the hospital. The camera ran out of film just as the limo disappeared under the underpass.

The assassination of President Kennedy stunned the nation. A rush of events followed: On Friday Vice President Lyndon Johnson was sworn in as president on the plane carrying Kennedy's body back to Washington. That same afternoon the assassin, Lee Harvey Oswald, was arrested in a Dallas movie theater. On Saturday, while it poured rain in Washington, the body of the president lay in state in the East Room of the White House. On Sunday, in front of live television news cameras, Oswald was shot dead in the police station by a nightclub owner named Jack Ruby. On Monday came the funeral itself, with the heart-wrenching image of JFK's small children mourning their dead father.

America's young were in shock. The president had formed a special bond with them, a bond that had helped them to feel that these times were particularly theirs. With his leadership gone, young people experienced a feeling of both freedom and responsibility. The decade now appeared to pass even more completely to them. A youth-oriented subculture emerged around the arrival of more sophisticated rock groups such as the Beatles, and a growing political awareness was centered around protest over American participation in the Vietnam War.

Vietnam, once the French colony of Indochina, had won its own war for independence in 1954. It ended with the country's being split into two halves: Communist North Vietnam and South Vietnam, which America would come to support. The war had also ended with an agreement that both North Vietnam and South Vietnam would hold elections on reunification. But when it became clear that the Communists would win the election, South Vietnam put off the referendum. Over the next few years, Vietnamese Communist guerrillas gradually infiltrated South Vietnam, eventually renewing the war.

Like Cuba, Vietnam was of little actual importance to the United States. But as with Cuba, Vietnam's embrace of Communism would be a serious blow to American prestige. And it was argued that if Vietnam became Communist, other nations in Asia might also fall under Soviet influence, like a tumbling row of dominoes. At first Americans gave their wholehearted support to South Vietnam in its struggle against the Communist North Vietnamese.

But in June 1963 several Buddhist monks burned themselves to death in protest against the brutally oppressive government of South Vietnam. Suddenly Americans began to wonder what they had gotten into. Perhaps the conflict in Vietnam was more complicated than it had seemed. Exactly what sort of government was the United States supporting in South Vietnam? As President Johnson intensified America's military presence with troops and arms, the antiwar movement intensified as well. For many of the young soldiers who went to Vietnam, the experience was baffling: They went into battle without really knowing what they were fighting for.

The way this war was fought was different, too. American GIs in Vietnam were not prepared to fight against smiling villagers who hid grenades behind their backs, or an army of snipers who fired on the Americans and then quickly dissolved into the jungle greenery. The GIs were supposed to be soldiers of democracy. But it wasn't at all clear that the government of South Vietnam had much support from its own people. What the people of Vietnam seemed to want most was a future free from domination by any foreign power, even the United States, which said it was trying to help them. For lack of any other cause, many American GIs fought for their fellow soldiers.

Larry Gwin, who was born in 1941, received a Silver Star for extraordinary heroism. He described the soldier's experience in Vietnam.

I arrived in Vietnam in July of '65. I landed with a group of soldiers on an airstrip just outside Saigon. Walking out of the airplane, the heat hit everyone in my entourage simultaneously, and everybody started to sweat. The roads into Saigon were dirt, and en route we passed homes which were nothing but tar paper and aluminum shacks with pigs and chickens in every yard. I thought, "This is the Third World." After an hour and a half, the school bus crossed a bridge into the teeming capital of Saigon. There were two traffic lights, and only one was functioning, so it was absolute bedlam between the jeeps, the trucks, the taxis, the buffalo carts, and the people on bicycles. Just before we pulled into headquarters, someone smashed a bottle against the bus. This person obviously didn't care about Americans and really didn't want us there. It was my first indication that maybe our presence wasn't quite as welcome as we had been led to believe.

I was sent to a base at An Khe to prepare for the arrival of fifteen thousand troops in mid-September. The troops arrived, and by early October had constructed a defensible perimeter around the base, and then we began our operations. On the afternoon of the fourteenth of November, we heard that the first battalion was engaged in heavy contact at a landing zone code-named X-ray in the Ia Drang Valley. My company was quickly sent in, in three waves of six helicopters each. We lifted up over the tall trees of our landing zone and we could see the clouds of smoke drifting from Chu Pong Mountain, where we were headed. I thought, "Oh, my God, we're not going to fly into that mess, are we?"

The helicopter set me down in the midst of chaos. There were air strikes against the mountain, and the *pop-pop-pop* of rounds in the air sounded like firecrackers. I saw three or four Americans huddled around a tree saying, "Get down, get down, man, they're all around us." I had been on the ground for all of ten seconds when a fellow jumped up next to me and said, "I'm hit, sir." Carrying our wounded guy, we dodged and weaved forward for about a hundred yards until we got to where we could see the battalion commander's post. In between there was nothing but burnt grass, where napalm had killed some people, stacks of empty ammo crates, and bent and broken weapons scattered around. There was a row of American dead covered with ponchos, but we had to spring past it and get ready to fight.

On the morning of November 17 we received orders to move to another landing zone about three miles due north. We knew there were North Vietnamese in the area. The temperature was maybe a hundred, and everybody was exhausted because we'd been awake for two days and were weighed down with our equipment. We set up in a clump of trees, waiting for the other platoons to go around and secure the area. All of a sudden we heard some shooting from the vicinity of our first platoon. After two or three single shots, the whole jungle opened up in one massive crescendo of fire. It seemed that everybody I knew and everybody behind us was firing every weapon they had. We had run into the North Vietnamese, and they had attacked us immediately.

I remember jumping up to go to a tree for some cover when the firing got bad, and as I was looking at the tree, right in front of my eyes, this chunk of wood came out at me, and I realized it was a bullet and that it had almost taken my nose off. I crunched down in the grass and ran back to where my company commander and radios were. The guys I was with were all down in the grass, hugging the dirt. Since I was lieutenant and had to know what was going on, I stuck my head up and saw about forty North Vietnamese soldiers coming across the grass at us. All I did was say, "Here they come," and start shooting at them. Everybody got the message and we cranked out a lot of fire, killing all the North Vietnamese. I remember those were the first men I ever killed, and I remember each one of them very distinctly. But if we hadn't killed them, they would have killed us. The Vietnamese came back that night and killed a lot of our wounded lying in the grass. Most everybody I knew was dead, and the stench of the battlefield was just unbelievable. It took us two days to clean up our dead and wounded and get us out of there.

We lost 70 percent of our men in the battle. General Westmoreland came down for Thanksgiving a week later to congratulate us on what he called our "distinguished victory," and as he did every one of us looked around and counted our losses. We thought, "Is *that* a victory, General?"

The Battle of Thanh Son 2 in May 1966 was a turning point for me. On the morning of May 6 we attacked a village complex surrounded by trees. We didn't really know what was behind the trees, because we followed a walking artillery barrage. It wasn't until we got to the site that we realized we had devastated a village, killing many civilians. We saw children and little kids with their legs blown off and old couples under smoking wreckage. It broke my heart, and it broke the hearts of the guys I served with. I know after we left that village, none of us could talk and none of us could look back.

There was no point during my year in Vietnam when I realized that the U.S. had made a mistake and that we shouldn't have been there. But I also know in my heart that any American soldier who went to Vietnam didn't have to stay there long before he knew that there was something wrong with our presence there, either by the look in the Vietnamese eyes or in the way that we were treating them or what we were doing in the countryside.

In 1964 Martin Luther King was awarded the Nobel Peace Prize. His efforts had helped convince Congress to pass the Civil Rights Act and the Voting Rights Act, and his moving speeches had brought many white Americans to his cause. But within the black community, impatience with the white establishment was growing, as well as impatience with King's turn-the-other-cheek leadership. Now, in the mid-sixties, other voices rose up, not from the

South but from the northern ghettos, asking: Why should we strive so hard to join a white community that doesn't welcome us? Why shouldn't we embrace our own heritage? The writings and teachings of Malcolm X offered a powerful alternative to King's message.

Malcolm X, born Malcolm Little (the X was his way of refusing the name given to his ancestors by white slaveholders), turned to the teachings of the black Muslim movement for guidance. He began to describe America in a deliberately provocative way, saying that southern whites were morally superior to northerners because at least they were honest about their racism. He mocked the image of the North as free. Preaching separation of the races, he urged African Americans to use the term *black* to describe themselves instead of the then common term *Negro*. Malcolm X's speeches set off alarm bells throughout white America.

"Black power" was the motto for activists who wanted to see more dramatic change in American society. To many, "black power" could only mean a black revolution intended to destroy the white establishment. With riots erupting in Los Angeles, Chicago, San Diego, Philadelphia, and other cities across the country, it looked as though the violent racial confrontation Americans had long feared might finally come. When Malcolm X was assassinated in 1965, his followers picked up his banner and carried it onward.

Kwame Turé, whose original name was Stokely Carmichael, was born in 1941. His experience demonstrated why Malcolm X found so many willing listeners.

I was with the first group to take trains from New Orleans as part of the Freedom Rides in 1961. It was a rough ride, because we were confronted by segregationists breaking train windows at every single stop until we got to Jackson, Mississippi, where the police arrested us for refusing to leave the white waiting room. We were sent to Hinds County Jail, and then, just to increase the pressure on us, a group of us were transferred to the Parchman Penitentiary on death row. The police were beating us and torturing us every night. I respected Martin Luther King for sticking to the nonviolence under all conditions, and I believed in it as long as it was effective, but if it wasn't working, then I decided that I would be throwing blows. By the time I walked out of Parchman Penitentiary, I was prepared to carry a gun in my work.

When I was growing up in Harlem, Malcolm X was there all the time, so I knew all about him and the Nation of Islam. Malcolm X presented a clearer, more direct political analysis, stripped of sentimentality, that saw the reality of the enemy we were fighting.

Since Malcolm X aimed his message directly at African Americans, he could touch us more deeply, while Martin Luther King's message also had to speak to white society. King would say, "What we need is morality," while Malcolm would say, "What we need is power." To Malcolm, nonviolence just meant that you're giving your cheek left and right to a man who has no conscience. He thought we needed an eye for an eye.

Malcolm X's assassination had a profound effect on us. After his assassination in 1965, those of us who really understood him made a conscious decision to pick up Malcolm's points and to build on them. We wanted to keep his philosophy alive. We decided to go into Lowndes County, Alabama, to use the vote as a means to organize the people. There was not one single black registered to vote there in 1965, yet 80 percent of the population in the county was black.

For three months before the arrival of election day, white terrorists sent out word that if any Africans went to vote, they'd be left there for dead. In order to encourage Africans to get out and vote, we let them know that young brothers and sisters were coming, armed, from the big cities to help out. I remember the Justice Department sent somebody to see me who said, "You know, your people are bringing in guns. What are you gonna do?" I said, "We're gonna vote." He said, "The whites are very upset about this." We had already decided that we would not fire the first shot, so I said, "You tell them they've got the first shot, but we're voting." When election day came, the people turned out to vote and not one shot was fired. For the first time, black citizens of Lowndes County felt they had exercised their political rights. They began to understand the power of politics.

Like much of America, Robert Kennedy, the former attorney general and now a U.S. senator, was changing his views on many different issues: the ongoing war in Vietnam, civil rights, the growing unrest among the country's young people. More and more people looked to him to challenge President Johnson to become the Democratic candidate in the 1968 presidential election. Many people were dissatisfied with the way Johnson had led the country since JFK's death. Eugene McCarthy, a senator from Minnesota who was against the war, was running for the Democratic Party's nomination, and in March of 1968 Bobby Kennedy also entered the race. Johnson, with so much of his own party against him, decided not to run again. Excitement was high; many Americans thought their troubles might be over if they could get another Kennedy into the White House.

But in 1968 it sometimes seemed as if every hope was destined to end in tragedy. In April Martin Luther King Jr. appeared in Memphis, Tennessee, in support of striking sanitation workers. There, on April 4, America's greatest prophet of nonviolence was shot and killed. When the news broke, violence erupted all over the country, with riots, arson, and gunfire. Though the deep anguish at King's death was heartfelt, the violence that followed was a sad tribute to a man who had dedicated his life to peaceful change.

Robert Kennedy was boarding a plane for a campaign stop in Indianapolis when he heard that King had been shot. He was scheduled to speak at a rally in Indianapolis's black ghetto, but when he arrived the chief of police told Kennedy the city could not guarantee his safety. Kennedy ignored the warning and went anyway. The crowd waiting for him did not know King had been killed. They gasped when Kennedy told them. Then he appealed to their best instincts. "You can be filled with bitterness, with hatred and a desire for revenge," he said. "We can move in that direction as a country. . . . Or we can make an effort, as Martin Luther King did . . . to replace that violence, that stain of bloodshed . . . with an effort to understand, with compassion and love." While the rest of the country burned, there were no riots in Indianapolis. There people took their grief home quietly. Two months later Bobby Kennedy, too, became the victim of an assassin's bullet.

College and university campuses were in an uproar, and not only in the United States. Students took to the streets in Paris and London. Czechoslovakia, a Communist country, had begun some modest but daring democratic reforms, nicknamed the "Prague Spring." But on August 20, 1968, some 650,000 Soviet troops marched into Czechoslovakia to force the country back into the Soviet camp. Mobs of Czech youths climbed onto Russian tanks and chanted, "USSR go home." But the Prague Spring was over.

The most notable American uprising came at the Democratic National Convention in Chicago. Ten thousand demonstrators traveled there to make their voices heard. Twenty-three thousand police officers and National Guard forces were waiting for them. An army of students faced off against an army of police in riot gear outside the convention center. Inside, party leaders nominated Johnson's vice president, Hubert Humphrey, as the Democratic candidate for president. The demonstrators outside claimed that the party leaders had ignored them and betrayed their hopes. It felt as if a civil war between America and its own young people had begun.

Jane Adams, born in 1943, was a member of Students for a Democratic Society who was in Chicago for the convention.

I had been active in the student Left throughout the sixties, but by 1968 I was so alienated from the political system that I was not following the processes of the Democratic candidates very closely. I remember many people saw Bobby Kennedy and Eugene McCarthy as hopeful forces for change, but after Martin Luther King's assassination, I began to feel that there was a rottenness at the core of the political system of this country.

I was a marshal out in the streets during the Democratic National Convention in Chicago. My most vivid memory of the convention was at the demonstration down at the McCarthy campaign headquarters. A crowd of thousands of people gathered outside, and the police were pushing us closer and closer together. Those of us who had experience protesting kept saying, "Stand up, stand up, stand up," because we knew the police were gonna charge and were gonna go in and slaughter them. After the police charged in, I saw this young man in a suit and tie and a woman who looked like she was a sorority girl, very well dressed, and she had blood pouring out of her hair. This young man had picked her up and was trying to push her in the door, and he was hysterical. I was so furious, because these kids were doing nothing.

When Humphrey was nominated, I was in the YMCA watching it on TV. I ran out in the streets, and armored personnel carriers with barbed wire on the front of them moved into position. The young people chanted, "The whole world is watching," which really meant that the whole world is watching this massive injustice that's going on here, the ripping off of our democracy from us.

On the night of July 20, 1969, Americans put away their anger. Along with billions of television viewers around the world, they watched as American astronaut Neil Armstrong stepped out of the lunar module and became the first man to walk on the moon.

The American space program had also been caught up in the Cold War struggle between democracy and Communism. After the Soviets had launched the *Sputnik* satellite in 1957, beating America into space, the United States had thrown its support behind NASA, the national space agency. JFK had pledged to put a man on the moon before the 1960s were over. Now, in 1969, that promise had been fulfilled.

Among those at the crowded Apollo XI launch site was the 1920s pilot Charles Lindbergh. It had been only forty-two years since his heroic flight across the Atlantic, but the world had changed a great deal. His had been an individual achievement; he had navigated his own plane through near disaster. The Apollo program was the work of billions of dollars of taxpayers' money and more than four hundred thousand people in assembly plants and control rooms.

Still, like Lindbergh's flight in the twenties, the mission of the three Apollo XI astronauts gave their wounded country something to be proud of, something to share. And when the nation's weary citizens saw pictures of their planet taken from space, they were moved: It was not the troubled world they knew, but a beautiful, peaceful globe, ordered and still.

CHAPTER 2

Years of Doubt

1969–1981

In the 1970s the booming postwar economy finally
went bust. There was no single event that announced this decline, nothing like the 1929 stock
market crash, which announced the arrival of the
Great Depression. Instead, high unemployment and
rising prices crept up on Americans. The unpopular
war in Vietnam and the crisis in the economy com-
bined to spread a feeling of mistrust of the government and its leaders. There was a new awareness
that the growth of industry had helped to damage
the environment. People worried about pollution,
overpopulation, inflation, and recession. The earth
itself, and the United States along with it, now
seemed fragile and the future uncertain.

Prices were going up and up, and the most painful price increase was the one at the gas pump. Oil was—and still is—the lifeblood of America. Every plane, tank, and car needs it. Every skyscraper and industrial plant runs on it. Oil is part of the fertilizer that helps farmers produce crops for the world; when used in drugs, it helps fight disease. Like no other raw material, oil created the American way of life. And it fueled the American dream machine, the automobile.

Since the 1920s the car had become a symbol of American prosperity. GM made big cars after World War II, and people bought them according to their status: the more successful you were, the bigger your car. For years America had been buying cheap oil from the petroleum-producing countries of the Middle East: Saudi Arabia, Iran, the United Arab Emirates, and others. But when America supported Israel in the 1973 Arab-Israeli War, the oil-producing countries punished the United States. They organized an oil embargo, cutting off America's pipeline.

Suddenly the price of gasoline and heating oil went up. Everything in the American economy that had depended on cheap energy got more expensive. People had to turn down their thermostats, cut back on driving, make do with less. A new thrift was force-fed to the country.

Long lines formed at gas stations, whose owners were asked to sell a maximum of ten gallons per customer. Now the large cars that Americans had been driving for so long were a handicap. Still, the powerful American automakers kept right on rolling big cars down the assembly lines. People began buying smaller, more fuel-efficient foreign cars instead. The era of the gas guzzler was over.

In Detroit the big automakers started laying off their workers. LaNita Gaines, born in 1950, was a Chrysler employee who watched as the oil crisis began hurting people's lives.

When I first started working at the plant, Chrysler was manufacturing these giant-sized cars. They had gigantic gas tanks and got little mileage, but they were big and comfortable. It seemed as if people were changing cars every two years, and they weren't really going for the quality of the car; they just wanted to keep up with the latest model. I swear at one point they were moving down the assembly line so fast that we'd sometimes miss a screw.

In 1973 we began to see a downturn in the industry as a whole. We workers would read about the oil crisis in the papers, and we didn't quite know what to make of it. All we knew is that people were waiting on seemingly endless lines to get a tank of gas, and Chrysler just kept building those huge cars. The public started paying closer attention to gas mileage and began turning to smaller, more fuel-efficient cars from abroad like the Germans' Volkswagen Beetle and Japanese cars. We had a Chrysler Imperial at that time, and it was a real gas-guzzler. We were getting eight miles to the gallon on it, and it seemed as if you could barely get from one gas station to the other before you had to fill up again. Eventually I had to say good-bye to it because I couldn't afford to keep gas in it.

The American companies were refusing to change to what was now going to be the new road for the auto industry. We workers just kind of looked at that and said, "Well, why don't they change? When are they gonna get the message that we're not in love with those big cars anymore?" We'd try to tell them that we were the ones that were buying those little cars, but the company didn't want to listen. We were looking for companies that made smaller cars, of course, that were American-made, but if America was not making those cars, then you had to buy what you could find. We had to get to work, we had to get our families around, and with gas prices climbing much faster than our wages, we had to do something. We had to buy what was economically feasible for our families.

I worked at Chrysler until around 1974. I had bought my first home and started a family. That November they came around and told us that we were permanently laid off. I was terrified. I thought, "What does this mean? I've had a job for all these years, and now I'm being put in the street." All of a sudden there was not enough money for the mortgage note and the car note. We could barely keep food on the table. I thought I could rely on unemployment for a while, but the industry had recently changed some of its policies in the cutbacks, so the sub fund, which was to help laid-off workers, was depleting quickly, and I realized there was just one step between me and the welfare line. There was a sentiment of despair everywhere. These were very shaky times, and we just didn't know what to do.

The faltering economy led many people to feel that their leaders were failing them. This disappointment in the government had really begun with Vietnam, a war Richard Nixon inherited from Democrat Lyndon Johnson when he became president in 1969. At first many Americans were pleased when Nixon set up a policy of "Vietnamization," which placed more of the burden of their own defense on the South Vietnamese, and started bringing American GIs home. But this good feeling did not last. In 1970 it was revealed that U.S. soldiers had massacred Vietnamese civilians at My Lai, and that same year the United States illegally invaded Cambodia. Protests against the war continued to divide the nation. In May four college students were killed by National Guard troops during an antiwar rally at Kent State University in Ohio. Rage and resentment seemed to be the only emotions Americans had in common.

The 1972 presidential campaign was under way when a seemingly minor crime took place. One night in June seven men broke into the offices of the Democratic National Committee in the Watergate office complex in Washington, D.C. The burglars were arrested. But when it was discovered that they were on the payroll of the Committee to Re-elect the President, a chain of events was set in motion that would eventually create a constitutional crisis known as Watergate. Americans watched with fascination and disgust as a complicated story of intrigue and obstruction of justice reached higher and higher in the government, eventually touching the president himself.

Hugh Sloan, born in 1940, was a White House aide who became caught up in the Watergate scandal.

I started working at the White House as an assistant to the president's appointment secretary during Nixon's first term in office. I was very young and driven, and it was exciting to see the inner workings of government. When election time neared I was put on a team to help organize the Committee to Re-elect the President. Working on the campaign was even more exciting than working at the White House. We were all working for a cause and by and large we were all believers, so there was a lot of enthusiasm around the office.

One morning I was in the office and I saw G. Gordon Liddy, who was in charge of campaign security, hurrying down the hall in a state of panic. As he ran by, I heard him say something like, "My boys got caught last night. I told him I'd never use anybody from here. I made a big mistake." I didn't know exactly what he was talking about at first, but it got me thinking. Then I read in the papers about the Watergate break-in, and I saw that James McCord was one of the people arrested. I knew McCord; he was directly involved in the Committee to Re-elect the President. The pieces fell together pretty quickly in my mind. It was obvious by the way everyone was acting around the office that the campaign was somehow involved in the break-in. The men who were arrested had a fair amount of cash on them, most of it new hundred-dollar bills. I suspected that cash might have come from money that I had given Liddy, purportedly for campaign security. All of a sudden I started wondering whether the investigators would be able to pick my fingerprints off of those bills.

As the Watergate situation ballooned, the atmosphere around the office became very bizarre. I couldn't get straight answers about anything. I told some people at the White House that there were real problems over here at the committee and that they needed to do something. But their reaction was to just turn their backs on it.

Next I talked to the two attorneys who had been hired by the campaign committee. They said that if what I was telling them [about the money] was accurate, then they'd been lied to by other people in the campaign. They were worried that I would be subpoenaed before they had time to deal with this, and they asked if I had any legitimate reason for being out of town. When I got home that night, Fred LaRue [the director of the re-election committee] called me and said that I should fly to California to help raise money for the campaign. He wanted to know if I could be on the morning plane from Dulles Airport [in Washington, D.C.]. And then he said, "Oh, by the way, could you spend the night at a motel near the airport so you won't be subpoenaed in the meantime?" So I did.

The next day on the flight I had a long time to think. Everything started to seem so crazy to me. Here I was, fleeing from the authorities. It was like I was a character in a movie. The lawyers for the campaign were there to protect the more senior people, and they weren't concerned about what happened to someone like me. Obviously I was in the chain of command that paid all of these people to do something that was illegal. The question was, would anybody know that I was not part of the conspiracy in the first place?

It was during that flight to California that I decided I could no longer work every day with people that were clearly trying to abort the investigation and, in essence, cover it up. I knew I would have to testify, and I felt an immense pressure to be as accurate as possible because I knew my testimony was going to have an impact on people's lives. I think the tragedy in all of this was that I saw a lot of young, enthusiastic people make terrible

> mistakes and get chewed up in the gears. Particularly people who had no direct involvement, but who perjured themselves to protect more senior people. So many people went to jail because they lied about the cover-up.

It is unlikely that President Nixon knew about the break-in itself. The attempt to cover it up afterward was the mistake that finally forced him to resign. And what Watergate revealed about the Nixon White House turned the public against him. Nixon had gathered around him a loyal group of advisers who followed orders without question. In the interest of serving the president they faked information, attempted to slander his opponents, tried to steal documents, and were involved in other "dirty tricks" that had become a way of life at the White House.

On August 8, 1974, Richard Nixon became the first president ever to resign his office. His vice president, Gerald Ford, was sworn in as the thirty-eighth president of the United States. Just four weeks later Ford issued a "full, free, and absolute" pardon to Richard Nixon, guaranteeing, to the disappointment of many, that the man who had brought such shame to America would never be asked to explain his part in the Watergate scandal.

Just six months after Nixon's resignation, South

Vietnam fell to the Communists. Americans watched the humiliating spectacle of marine helicopters taking off from the roof of the U.S. embassy in Saigon, leaving desperate South Vietnamese friends behind. It was yet another blow to American pride. Now, with the defeat of South Vietnam, America had undeniably lost a war. Fifty thousand American soldiers had died for nothing.

The collapse of faith in American leadership and the defeat in Vietnam further undermined Americans' self-confidence. People responded by turning inward and becoming more focused on themselves. Instead of identifying themselves as Americans, many people began to think of themselves as members of groups with particular interests and rights. Many people now saw themselves first as women, or Latinos, or senior citizens, or environmentalists. The population seemed to be separating into special-interest groups, each fighting for its own cause.

Women were by far the largest and most successful of these groups. Feminist claims to equal rights had begun in the days of the suffragist movement. By the 1960s, the light cast by the civil rights movement made it increasingly obvious that African Americans weren't the only ones being denied equal opportunity.

In 1962 Betty Friedan had published a landmark book called *The Feminine Mystique*. In it she gave voice to the powerful but hard-to-explain feeling that so many women shared: that there was something missing from their lives, that motherhood and housework alone did not nourish the spirit or bring fulfillment. In 1966 Friedan established the National Organization for Women (NOW), which quickly focused on two main goals: the Equal Rights Amendment (ERA) and the right to safe, legal abortion.

In 1972 Congress passed the Equal Rights Amendment. And in 1973 the Supreme Court ruled in favor of abortion rights in a landmark case called *Roe v. Wade*. While both of these victories would come under severe attack (the ERA was never ratified by the states), they signaled an important shift in the way American society viewed women. Many people began to take another look at the traditional roles of men and women. Why were girls always sent to home economics classes while boys were assigned to shop classes? Shouldn't boys learn to cook? Shouldn't girls know how to use tools? Why was it always the husband who worked and the wife who raised the children? Couldn't women be the family breadwinners? Couldn't fathers stay home to take care of the kids?

But these questions also awoke a backlash against some aspects of feminism. By using the same argument that had been used against suffragists— the idea that rights for women would destroy the family—conservatives encouraged an antifeminist campaign. The issue that brought the emotions of both sides to a fever pitch was abortion. To many feminists, abortion was the most fundamental of rights, the right of a woman to control her own body and her own health. By contrast, their conservative and religious opponents saw abortion as an act of human arrogance, an attempt to replace the will of God with the will of the individual.

For many women, the goals of the women's movement—equal pay for equal work, affordable child care for working mothers, the ability to control their reproductive lives—were very close to home. Marie Wilson, born in 1940, was typical of the women who began to demand change.

I was quite certain that after college I'd marry, have children, stay at home, and have this great life that I saw in the Betty Crocker ads. But I was living in a very interesting time, sort of on the cusp between two eras. Half of me wanted to do something different, but half of me felt loyal to this vision of life as a wife and mother. So when my boyfriend proposed to me in 1962, I decided to drop out of college and marry him, but then I immediately changed my mind and canceled the wedding, deciding to go to graduate school instead. Just as suddenly I changed my mind again and had the wedding after all. Within nine months I was pregnant with my first child.

I felt like things had gone badly for my mother because she had to work outside the home, but it would be different for me, I thought, because I would stay home and be a happy, loving, perfect mother. Of course, things didn't happen that way. My husband and I moved around a lot and I didn't have a very good support system, so I was home alone with the baby quite a lot. I started to feel like you would feel on an airplane when they tell you the mask is going to drop and that you should just breathe normally. You can't breathe normally with a child in an apartment, without a lot of money, without friends and family. Children aren't meant to be raised in a home with just one adult who never leaves the house. I didn't like it. And I was also disappointed with myself for not absolutely loving this motherhood experience.

I got pregnant again—my fourth time in four and a half years. I had been sick a lot during those years—my body was just worn out—and I remember sitting in the bathtub and crying. I asked myself, "What am I gonna do? I really can't deal with having that many children, and the only alternative is abortion. Can I risk getting an illegal abortion?" There was a good chance then that I could die from it, and I didn't want to leave my children motherless. It suddenly hit me that something was wrong with this picture. For the first time, I realized I had been working for African American rights, for peace in Vietnam, but that I still had no choices, nor any peace, in my personal life.

The push for women's rights in this country really was a kitchen-table movement, started by women like me who needed changes in their lives. I found a number of women out there who felt the same way I did, and we started working together in our homes. Everything we wanted in life—whether it was to choose how many children to have, to go back to school, to get involved in the workforce—we were determined to go out and create in the world. So we gathered around kitchen tables and pieced together legislation, wrote petitions, and planned events while our children ran around the room. We figured out who to write to in the legislature in order to pass the Mondale child-care bill in the early seventies. I remember working on the Mondale bill, talking to a labor economist in my kitchen; I had a child in one hand, and I was stirring spaghetti sauce with the other.

Meanwhile, the media was creating a movement that was unrecognizable to me—people who burned bras, who hated men and all of that. I had no idea who these people were, what they did, what they looked like. That branch of the movement was never something I could identify with. My feminism came straight out of my own circumstances. I needed to space my children, so I worked on [reproductive] choice. I needed child care in order to work, so I worked on child care. I needed a better job, so I worked on creating good work for women. It wasn't about a national movement. It was simply something that was happening to me, to my friends, to my community. That was feminism.

Arguments over the future of the environment, like the battles over feminism, occupied Americans more and more in the 1970s. Once it had seemed as though there was no limit to America's material progress. Factories had produced an endless stream of products. The land had produced enough food to feed the country and export the surplus around the world. But the image of the earth seen from the Apollo XI moon landing had given Americans a new perspective, one of a vulnerable planet that had been contaminated by people and industry.

Many Americans began to question their way of life: Was mass consumption morally right? They also began to question science: Had technology been exploiting natural resources without considering the consequences? Americans looked around and noticed what they had done to their own country: pollution, toxic-waste dumps, poisoned rivers, and endangered species.

In March 1979 the nation's attention was riveted on a nuclear power plant in Pennsylvania: Three Mile Island. A nuclear accident had brought the plant dangerously close to a meltdown. The sense of science gone awry filled people's minds with frightening images of birth defects and cancers. There was a growing belief that American prosperity was risking the health of the earth itself.

Lois Gibbs, who was born in 1951, personally suffered the consequences of the industrial machine. She and her family lived in Love Canal, a small town in upstate New York where people mysteriously began to get sick.

When I moved to Love Canal, in 1972, I felt I had achieved the American dream: I had a husband with a good job, a healthy one-year-old child, a station wagon, and my very first house, which even had a picket fence. I was living in a thriving community directly across from the mighty Niagara River. Everything in Love Canal seemed to be meant for families. We felt it was just the perfect neighborhood.

Then my son, Michael, got very sick. When we moved into our house, he was one year old and perfectly healthy. Then he developed skin problems, asthma, epilepsy, a liver problem, an immune system problem, and a urinary tract disorder. When I asked the pediatrician what was going on, he told me, "You just must be an unlucky mother with a sickly child." My second child, Melissa, who was conceived and born at Love Canal, at first seemed to be perfectly healthy. Then one Friday I noticed bruises on her body. On Saturday the bruises were larger. And by Sunday the bruises on my little girl's body were the size of saucers. She looked like a child abuse victim! I took her to the pediatrician, but he didn't know what was wrong. He just took a blood test and sent us home. Later that afternoon he called and said, "Mrs. Gibbs, I believe your daughter has leukemia." We had no family history of any of these types of illnesses. It just didn't make any sense to me why my kids were so sick.

Around that time articles started appearing in the *Niagara Falls Gazette* that talked about hazardous waste in dump sites all across the city of Niagara Falls. Then I read one article that talked about a dump next to the Ninety-ninth Street Elementary School, where my son attended kindergarten. In this article they listed the chemicals that were buried there and what could result from exposure to these chemicals. I literally checked off every single one of my children's diseases and said to myself, "Oh, my God. It's not that I am an unlucky mother. My children are being poisoned." I couldn't believe that somebody would build a school next to a dump site.

I found out that other people were going through the same thing I was. One person had a thirteen-year-old daughter who had to have a hysterectomy due to cancer. There were eight other epileptics living in houses that practically encircled ours. And it wasn't just children who were sick; adults were getting sick as well. People would walk me down to their basement and show me orange goo coming up from their sump pumps. In some homes the chemical smell was so strong that it was like walking into a gas station.

In the spring of 1978 the state department of health came in and did some tests around Love Canal. And then they denied, denied, denied, and denied from that point on. They told the people living closest to the canal, "Don't go in your basement. Don't eat out of your garden. Don't do this, don't do that, but it's perfectly safe to live at Love

Canal." We did our own house survey. And we found that 56 percent of the children at Love Canal were born with birth defects. And that included three ears, double rows of teeth, extra fingers, extra toes, or mentally retarded.

Before Love Canal, I believed that if you had a problem, you could just go to your elected officials and they would fix it. I now know that that's not true. The state didn't do anything until we forced it to. Eventually nine hundred families were evacuated from Love Canal. But what outraged me the most was that a state health department knew people were sick, knew people were dying, and decided to do nothing about it.

There were many things that worried Americans in the 1970s: rising oil prices, high unemployment, toxic waste, untrustworthy government, a crumbling international reputation, and the breakdown of traditional gender roles. But in 1979 one unfolding drama in a Middle East nation closed out the decade with a new and ferocious attack on American pride.

Once again, Cold War fears had led America to become involved in the affairs of a Third World country. Iran, which was a southern neighbor of the Soviet Union, was considered strategically important because it was so rich in the oil that America needed. For years the United States had supported the shah of Iran as a way of maintaining its influence there. But, as in South Vietnam, a government that was opposed to Communism proved to be anything but democratic.

Within Iran, anger at America's interference had been growing steadily. As Muslims, its people resented the pressure to give up their traditions and embrace American materialism. They had been listening to the words of an exiled Muslim cleric, Ayatollah Khomeini. Khomeini taught the lessons of the Shari'a, the seventh-century Islamic law, and denounced the modernization forced on Iran by the shah. In early 1979 the shah was overthrown in an Islamic revolution that brought Khomeini to power.

The revolution in Iran was a rejection of much that the United States stood for. The Ayatollah Khomeini and the religious leaders now in power in Iran saw American culture as lacking moral fiber, a civilization that had grown fat and weak. And with Iran's oil fields in the grip of a hostile power, prices rapidly rose, impressing upon people just how dependent the United States was on foreign oil. But it wasn't until later in the year that the Iranian revolution became a personal issue for most Americans.

On November 4, Iranian students loyal to Khomeini cut the chains on the gates of the American embassy in the capital city of Teheran. They stormed past marine guards and took sixty-six members of the embassy staff hostage. They demanded the return to Iran of the shah, who was in New York City undergoing cancer treatment.

With mounting horror, Americans watched the evening news to see what would happen. American hostages were paraded blindfolded in front of television cameras by students who burned American flags and shouted "Death to America!" Calling the United States "the Great Satan," they declared that Americans were their mortal enemies.

President Jimmy Carter seemed helpless to end the crisis. Khomeini considered himself a messenger from God and refused to negotiate. Military threats wouldn't work, for the militant Islamic revolutionaries were willing to die for their cause. "Why should we be afraid?" asked a defiant Khomeini. "We consider martyrdom a great honor." For 444 days Americans waited, tying yellow ribbons on trees across the nation as a symbol that the hostages were not forgotten.

Barry Rosen, born in 1944, was one of the hostages who endured the long ordeal.

In the months before the shah left Iran you could see a tremendous deterioration of the government's power. The Iranian people were up in arms. Every night I would hear shouting on the rooftops, "*Allah hu akbar! Marg bar shah!* God is great, down with the shah!" I would walk around and then report what was going on back to the United States embassy. Sometimes, of course, I'd get rifle butts stuck in my back and people would tell me to move on. But I could feel it, sense it, smell it—the regime was falling. The day the shah finally left was one of the most potent and vivid days imaginable. It's difficult to fully understand just how much the Iranian people hated him. And then when Khomeini returned, ecstatic crowds carried him through the streets of Teheran. It was as if the Messiah had landed.

To me, November 4, 1979, seemed like just an ordinary gray, rainy Sunday in Teheran. I was at work at ten o'clock that morning. All of a sudden I heard marching sounds coming from the main avenue in Teheran. I looked out my window and saw Iranian students climbing the gates and jumping over the walls of the embassy. They had photographs of Khomeini on their chest and they were yelling, "*Marg bar Amrika!* Death to America!" The students banged on my door, and then came storming in with clubs and some small arms.

We were taken to a library in the embassy, where the hostage takers interrogated me and my Iranian coworkers. They eventually let all the Iranians go. I had become good friends with the Iranians in my office, and I cried because I was happy that they were being let go. They cried because they were sure that I was going to be executed. I was tied up and blindfolded and then led out of the library into the courtyard, raindrops hitting me on the head. That's when I started to think about my family, and I began to wonder, "Will I live through the rest of the night?"

My captors dragged me into the cook's quarters, where they took off my shoes and started searching them, trying to tear the heels apart. They thought that I had some secret message machine in the heels of my shoes. They were convinced that we were all CIA agents and would do anything to escape. That's why they tied us up day in and day out.

One of the most wrenching moments in my captivity was when the students tried to get me to sign a letter indicating my crimes against Iran. This young man held an automatic weapon to my head and started to count down from ten to one. It was then that I realized that I would do anything to survive. I wanted to be a good American, and I didn't want to sign something that would state that I was not, but I knew that the best thing to do to survive was to sign whatever needed to be signed, so I did.

The worst pain of it all was brought on by the length of captivity. Not the boredom, but the fear that grows inside of you over a long period of time. The fear of death. A fear that creeps into the subconscious. That, and just not being able to go outside, to see a bird fly, or to take a walk. The physical cruelty, getting beaten up or being pushed around or being blindfolded, was less of a potent force than the lack of freedom.

There was no other alternative but to live. I spent several months sharing a room with a lieutenant colonel named Dave Roeder. He was a man who knew how to survive. He taught me to get up and exercise and to meet each day with purpose. We learned to make small things beautiful. For example, for whatever weird reason, the Iranians gave me the classifieds from the *Washington Post* boat section. Not great reading, but something. Dave actually knew something about boats, so he would describe the different types, and we would both lie down on the floor and we would take a trip on the Chesapeake Bay. Just escaping in our imaginations like that made life worthwhile.

One morning in January a guard came in and said, "Pack your bags. You're leaving." Just like that. Once again we were bound and blindfolded and then marched to a bus.

We traveled on the bus for what seemed like an interminable amount of time. When it finally stopped, they ripped off my blindfold and pushed me out of the bus. I stumbled past this long line of Iranian guards who spat on me. I was just soaking wet from spit. But I saw this light and an arm waving toward me. It turned out to be the entrance of an Air Algiers plane, so I ran toward it. It seemed so unreal. It was as if we were in another world altogether—very blurred, but once we realized we were free, also very beautiful.

Back in the United States we were greeted as heroes. We were so isolated that we didn't realize that we had become the center of the American news, that we had been their purpose for the last 444 days. In some ways, I think the people were celebrating what they believed was American power. But I honestly think that both countries lost. There was a lot of hate on both sides that didn't need to happen. I don't believe we were winners. I believe it was a period of great sadness.

The hostage crisis continued through the 1980 presidential campaign. Americans were exhausted by disappointment, turmoil, and embarrassment. They wanted to feel good about themselves again. And they elected as president a man who promised to let them do that and to bring the country back to a golden age. That man was Ronald Reagan. In his inaugural address in 1981 Reagan asked Americans to believe once again in their capacity for greatness. And as he spoke the weary hostages were being dragged into the night and pushed aboard an airplane bound for home. The long national nightmare was over.

CHAPTER 3

New Morning

1981–1989

Americans entered the 1980s worn by the events of the previous decade. They longed for a fresh start, and they found it in a new, conservative approach to government. The leader of this conservative "revolution" was the new president, Ronald Reagan.

Ronald Reagan was the most influential president in forty years. Anger over high inflation and the Iranian hostage crisis had pushed Americans to vote President Carter out of office. Reagan, a former actor and governor of California, rallied the nation with nostalgic images of less complicated times. He called upon Americans to return to the values of hard work and self-reliance that had made their country great. To some, Reagan's foreign policy ideas sounded simplistic and extreme, and his economic policies seemed to blame the poor for their own problems. But his message of good feeling and self-confidence seemed to invigorate the nation.

Richard Viguerie, born in 1933, shared the enthusiasm many Americans felt about President Reagan.

Ronald Reagan was the epitome of America. He was an optimist and a "can-do" type of leader. He believed that today is great, but tomorrow's going to be better. In times of crisis, Reagan was able to reach out to the American people and put his arms around us and bring us together. He was always recognized as the "Great Communicator." The reason Ronald Reagan was such an effective speaker was because he had a message that resonated with America.

It was no accident that, literally a few minutes after Reagan became president, the hostages were freed. I think that if Carter had been reelected, those hostages would have been there throughout Carter's presidency, because Khomeini knew he had somebody that he could move around like a puppet on a string. But Ronald Reagan had sent a very clear message, which is the old New Hampshire state message—Don't Tread on

Me. The Iranians weren't 100 percent sure of Ronald Reagan and they weren't gonna take any chances.

Ronald Reagan moved boldly and decisively. The major world leaders saw that they were dealing with a man of strength and that the rules had been changed from the Nixon-Ford-Carter days. They were now dealing with an administration that was going to stand up for its beliefs and its rights. Mr. Reagan had an agenda, and he knew where he was going.

Like Franklin Delano Roosevelt before him, Ronald Reagan was a master communicator. He made people feel that something was getting done. Unlike Roosevelt, however, Reagan did not see the power of the state as a positive tool to help society. He believed that oversize government programs had made people weak and dependent. Where Roosevelt had wanted to save people *with* government, Reagan wanted to save people *from* government.

The essence of Reagan's economic policy was the tax cut. His philosophy was that people who made money should be allowed to keep it. And if the rich had money to spend, it would eventually "trickle down" to the people who had less. This argument allowed him to cut funding for social programs that had been constructed to aid the poor.

At the same time that Reagan cut taxes, he also increased defense spending. His view of the Soviet Union was simple: It was an "evil empire" and must not be coddled. He dramatically enlarged America's supply of nuclear weapons. But with less money coming into the government from taxes and more money going into defense, the federal budget became seriously out of balance.

Nonetheless, the economy seemed to be on the mend. America's standing in international affairs, thanks to Reagan's tough, no-nonsense attitude toward the Soviets, was improving. But all was not rosy. Reagan's trickle-down theory had justified severe cuts in social spending, but the trickling was hard to see. Many people enjoyed the new prosperity, but at the bottom of the ladder, others were falling into deep trouble.

The Reverend Patrick Mahoney, born in 1954, saw a tragedy emerging from President Reagan's economic policies.

What was discouraging to me about President Reagan was that he was the first style-over-substance president. He had great style in front of the public up there, but he was lacking in substance. For example, he talked about church values, but he never went to church. He talked about family values, yet he had an incredibly dysfunctional family and his children didn't talk to him. He spoke out about drugs, but we saw cocaine wars in south Florida. He wanted to reduce government spending, yet the deficit sky-rocketed. President Reagan introduced something very detrimental, and that is this photo-op kind of candidacy. It dumbed down the political debate and made everybody more interested in good sound bites and creative commercials than in real issues.

Also Reagan's economic policies made life very difficult for a lot of people. The theory behind Reaganomics was that the rising tide would lift up all the boats. If the already well-to-do started making more money, then it would trickle down to the less well-off and everyone would do better. But in reality that was not the case. I lived in Bristol, Connecticut, in the 1980s. And under Reagan, Bristol experienced this huge boom. I mean, it was great. Everyone was saying, "Aren't things wonderful? Aren't things just spectacular under President Reagan? He's our man. He's lowered interest rates. I'm making money hand over fist." But that was for people who owned property and who were already fairly well off. For people who didn't have money—for the poor—it was a horrible time. Property values in Bristol doubled or tripled, but so did the rents. And as the rents went up, the wages of the working class stayed the same, and suddenly many people couldn't afford to live in their own homes anymore. In Bristol, as in a lot of America, entire families found themselves without a home. These were not lazy people. They were not sluggards or substance abusers. They were committed, dedicated men and women who were trying to make a difference in their own life, and suddenly they couldn't afford a place to live.

So when I hear about the legacy of Mr. Reagan, and I hear of the good times of the Reagan years, I can say that I personally benefited—the value of my home more than tripled—but the same factors that allowed for me to make money turned out to be very hard on the working class. The trickle-down theory just stopped at those who already had money, and many of those who were already struggling to make ends meet were forced out into the streets. It was tragic.

For the poor, life was getting harder. Homelessness was on the rise. So were drug abuse and the crime that came with it. But the Reagan era encouraged many to distance themselves from these social problems. The social consciousness of the sixties and seventies now seemed to have faded, a victim of impatience, cynicism, and, for some, a firm belief that government programs rarely worked. At the top of the ladder of opportunity, some wealthy Americans spent their newly made money more freely and publicly on themselves.

Starting in 1982, more than a hundred thousand new millionaires were created each year, so many that the word *millionaire* lost its significance. Millionaire? Try billionaire. America was throwing itself into conspicuous consumption: big cars, mammoth houses, opulent dinners, and luxurious vacations. The panting pursuit of wealth was now acceptable, even admirable. "Greed is good," claimed a character in *Wall Street,* a movie that defined the times.

Chris Burke, born in 1958, experienced the excitement of easy money on Wall Street in the 1980s.

In 1979 I was two years out of high school and working in a local bar in Manhasset, Long Island, a bedroom community for people who work in Manhattan. And probably about 80 percent of those people worked on Wall Street. A lot of these Wall Street guys were regulars at the bar and they were always saying things like "What are you doing here? Come on down and work on Wall Street with us. You have what it takes." They made it all seem very glamorous, and I was lured in. In 1980 I went down to work on the floor of the New York Stock Exchange. Wall Street was just heading into a big upswing, so things were pretty exciting down there. Suddenly there I was, a twenty-year-old kid with a high-school education, and I was starting out at $40,000 a year.

I was a clerk for a specialist house that traded in about eighty big stocks like TWA, Delta Air Lines, things like that. I stood behind a counter, and outside the counter was the broker I worked for. Surrounding him were ten to twenty guys just screaming and yelling, buying and selling. And I'd have to record all of these orders. Hectic isn't the word. It was overwhelming. We ripped our hair out of our head for the entire day every day.

When the bell rang in the afternoon, we cleaned up, and then it was cocktail time. I went out every night with the guys that I worked with and our immediate bosses. And we never spent a penny. Everything was on an expense account. We would go to this same restaurant a couple of blocks from the stock exchange. There'd be about fifteen guys. And we'd head right for the bar and just start pounding drinks. Then we'd sit down at the table. And we'd never even see a menu; the food would just start to come out, and it seemed like it would never end. It was obscene. Platters and platters of food and bottles and bottles of wine. We never thought once about what anything cost. Not at all. Just like at the exchange, it was all funny money. Never your money. So you didn't think about it.

In 1982 I switched over to the government bond market. By the mid-1980s the government bond market was booming and I was making good money with a nice bonus every year. I bought a new house, new cars, new clothes, and I became so entrenched in the lifestyle that I was spending tons of money. When your whole life revolves around money, pretty soon your value judgments come into question. My buddies and I would literally be stepping over homeless people on our way to work, and we'd snicker about it. We certainly didn't want to get our shoes scuffed up by their burlap pants. "Get a job" was our attitude.

Wall Street in the 1980s was like nowhere else on this planet. It was a culture of greed and backstabbing and partying. Your best buddy is the one who's gonna stab you in the back tomorrow if it means some more greenbacks in his pocket. It wasn't a good way to live, but it was the only way I knew.

Not since the Roaring Twenties had there been such a culture of money and glitz in America. Yet the new rich were making money differently than their predecessors. A thriving 1920s capitalist might have amassed a fortune building automobiles, while a successful 1950s businessman might have thought up new ways to sell products. In the 1980s millionaires were often lawyers and investment bankers who got rich not by *building* or *selling* anything, but by shifting ownership of companies, by refinancing companies, by making deals. It was all done on paper, and to many it all felt a little unreal.

Looking back, experts would agree that this was a streamlining that American business desperately needed. Still, all this wheeling and dealing, which seemed so abstract, affected the jobs—and the lives—of real people. Sometimes it meant closing factories in the United States and reopening them in places such as Thailand or Mexico. Why should management pay union workers in Ohio or Michigan high wages when they could pay a tenth of that to someone in the Third World? Sometimes it meant buying out local family-owned businesses to break them apart and sell each part.

Whole towns suffered dramatically from this rampage of mergers, acquisitions, and relocations. Communities that had relied on local factories for jobs now found themselves without any source of employment. Increasingly, people could not find new jobs. A new underclass emerged. Most visible were the homeless, people living on the street, whose desperate lives seemed to put the lie to claims that the country was back on its feet. The homeless problem was a complicated one, caused in part by Reagan's welfare cuts, by an inner-city drug epidemic, by a shortage of affordable housing, and by the decline of marriage, which left more people struggling to get by on their own.

A powerful new form of cocaine, called "crack," swept through American cities in the late 1980s. Darryl McDaniels, born in 1964, is the "DMC" of the rap group Run-DMC. He saw the damage crack did to his community.

I grew up on the tree-lined streets of Hollis, Queens, in New York. Most of the parents in my neighborhood were hardworking people with nine-to-five jobs. You knew everybody's parents, every kid, every uncle, the name of every dog and cat on the block, and the TV repairman, the oil man, and the mailman. Hollis was really a close-knit middle-class community. Almost every Saturday in the summer, the whole neighborhood would come into the park, and a DJ would be there, and the rappers and the emcees from the neighborhood would come on the set and we'd rap and we'd party and we'd DJ and we'd play music and have fun until the police came and said, "Somebody called the cops on y'all. Y'all gotta go home."

In the early eighties I started noticing neighborhood businesses were closing down. Our favorite candy store and deli, where we'd go as kids to read comic books, closed. The supermarket kept closing and reopening under a new name. The crime level was going up a little bit. People, particularly older people and well-educated people, started moving out of Queens, too. Even when we'd DJ in the park, fewer and fewer people were coming.

So the neighborhood was already starting to go downhill when I left to do a tour from 1984 to 1986. My rap group, Run-DMC, had made it big with our first single. Everywhere we went on tour, and especially in the South, people were talking about this new drug called crack. And we'd see crack fiends on the road and we could see how it hooked people. But we didn't realize crack had penetrated so deep into our own neighborhood.

I came off the tour in 1986 and went home to Hollis. I remember walking around and noticing how desolate everything had become. I looked at the playground, and the bleachers were gone. All the signs were ripped off, and there were holes in the fence and glass and rubbish and garbage all through it. The place looked like a war zone.

I was walking around one afternoon when I heard a woman say, "Darryl!" I turned around and I couldn't figure out who this person was. "It's me," she said. She said her name, and I realized she was my good friend's sister. She may as well have pulled out a gun and shot me, I was so stunned. It was obvious she was using crack, but she was trying to hold a regular conversation as if nothing was wrong. How was I supposed to react when she looked like she weighed about ten pounds? She had lost all her teeth and her clothes were dirty. I had held her as a baby. But now to see her like that, it was really scary.

Everyone's sister seemed to be getting addicted to crack. But when I started hearing about people's mothers, I just couldn't believe it. You'd look at the babies and wonder why they were like that. And it was because the parents were cracked out. I never knew that a drug could have such an impact on a community or a society. Every week something happened, whether it was somebody getting killed or arrested or dying. It was as if the whole neighborhood started disappearing. It became like a ghost town.

At the time everything in the neighborhood was falling apart, a lot of billboards saying Say No to Drugs were going up. I remember thinking how much money it cost to put up those signs each week. To me, they were spending money on the wrong thing. I knew perfectly well that people weren't gonna look at a sign like that and say, "All right, I'm gonna just say no to drugs." I found out that just telling people not to do drugs doesn't work. Besides, that saying came a little bit too late. Don't you think, Mr. Reagan?

As the gap between the haves and the have-nots got wider, America sometimes felt like a colder, crueler place. Beneath the glitzy surface ran a chilling current of fear. There was fear of crime, certainly, but also fear of failure, of not "making it" in the rush for riches. The nuclear arms race between the United States and the Soviet Union had intensified, bringing back fears of nuclear devastation. In 1986 an explosion destroyed the nuclear reactor at the Chernobyl power plant in the Soviet Union. A radioactive cloud spread for miles, contaminating the region's soil, crops, and livestock and renewing fears of a nuclear power plant accident in the United States.

But the most paralyzing event of the decade happened in Florida on January 28, 1986. The space shuttle *Challenger* was ready for launch, and it was carrying a very special passenger. Christa McAuliffe, a social studies teacher from Concord, New Hampshire, was about to become the first private citizen in space. Her flight would mark the beginning of a new age of civilian space travel, in which space would be open to everyone. NASA planned to have McAuliffe teach two fifteen-minute classes from the space shuttle, which would be beamed by television to millions of students across America.

It was unusually cold at Cape Canaveral that morning, but not cold enough to cancel the flight. The liftoff seemed to go smoothly, but seventy-three seconds later *Challenger* erupted into a fiery red ball. The space shuttle had exploded, killing everyone on board. For the nation's schoolchildren, it was the end of a dream.

Malcolm McConnell, born in 1939, was at Cape Canaveral to cover the *Challenger* launch for *Reader's Digest.*

Before I witnessed my first shuttle launch, NASA officials escorted several other reporters and me down to the launchpad to see the shuttle up close. I felt like an ant walking around a stepladder. I felt awed and dwarfed by this huge machine. When you're three miles away in the press grandstand and that huge assembly lights itself on fire and takes off, the feeling is overpowering. There is a bright flash from the solid rocket boosters, and then you see an almost volcanic burst of steam from the main engines. Immediately after the flash this huge vehicle begins to rise away, and it's all silent. A second or two later you are literally assailed by the shock waves. The press grandstand has sort of a tin metal roof that begins to bounce up and down, and your chest is hit by this cacophonous pounding. The first time I saw it, I was virtually speechless. I felt proud that my country, my civilization, had put together this wonderful machine which was so powerful, so complex.

By the mid-1980s NASA had pretty well convinced most of the world not only that it could run the space shuttle economically, but that the shuttle could actually pay for itself on a commercial basis. NASA wanted to prove that the shuttle was so safe that even an ordinary person could ride into space. So Christa McAuliffe, a high-school social studies teacher from New Hampshire, was to encourage an interest in space for millions of schoolchildren.

The morning the *Challenger* was launched, very few of us who had covered the space shuttle program thought it was going to fly that day. It was bitterly cold. One reporter pointed up at one of the monitors and said, "Look at the ice." The launch tower looked like a frozen waterfall. But we got our coffee and we sat around and waited. As it got light, the launch control people began saying, "Well, it's looking better and better." NASA had somehow pulled this thing off. And then the countdown reached five, four, three, two, one, and that glare lit up from the solid rocket boosters. I had a sense of great pleasure and satisfaction.

As the shuttle cleared the tower and the first shock waves of sound began to pound the press grandstand, I had my first sense of foreboding. Because the air was so cold and dense, the pounding sound was much louder than I'd ever experienced. I thought, "That does not sound right." But I quickly shrugged it off as the shuttle rose. All of us on the grandstand were screaming our heads off, yelling, "Go! Go!" Any sense of professional composure was lost; we were all caught up in the euphoria of the moment.

The pillar of smoke with the little tiny shuttle had turned to the degree so we could no longer see the shuttle itself. We could just see the rippling cloud of white and orange smoke coming back toward us. From our vantage point, it still looked like a normal flight. Then there was silence. For a long time. I would say ten seconds, which is a long time during a launch. And we began looking around at each other. And then the voice came over the loudspeakers. In a very dry, almost emotionless voice, "Obviously a major malfunction. We have no down-link. . . ." And then there was a pause. "The flight dynamics officer reports that the vehi-cle has exploded." I felt this terrible cold drenching doom pouring over me. I could al-most feel ice water pouring down over my head and chilling me deep into myself. Look-ing around me, I saw people who had been standing and cheering a moment before sink back down to their benches. Many people put their hands over their faces as if to blot out the sight. Other people put their hands to their throats, as if they themselves were being physically assaulted. One of my col-leagues looked at me and asked, "What's happened? Where are they?" I said, "They're dead. We've lost them, God bless them." And she got angry. She kind of pushed me and said, "Stop kidding. What happened? Where are they?" And I said, "They're dead.

They're dead." And at that moment we looked up again, and the pieces of the *Challenger* began tumbling out of that pillar of smoke. That massive vehicle had been shredded into tiny little pieces that were falling like confetti out of the sky.

Fear was also stalking America in the form of a new and deadly disease. For years medical science had been scoring one success after another. Its achievements promised to make human life better than ever. Then came the AIDS epidemic. AIDS stands for "acquired immunodeficiency syndrome." First detected in the early 1980s, it was believed to be a "gay disease." Homosexual men were being struck down by a mysterious onslaught of unusual infections that their bodies could not fight off. Before long, AIDS was also diagnosed in intravenous drug users, prostitutes, hemophiliacs, and some immigrants from Haiti and Africa. Because there was no clear understanding of what this deadly disease was, how it spread, or how to treat it, fear and hysteria quickly swept much of the nation.

For more than a decade, activists had been struggling for gay rights, and they had made considerable progress. But the arrival of AIDS brought a backlash against the gay community. Some conservative critics went so far as to claim that AIDS was God's revenge against "immoral" people. All the finger-pointing and name-calling often hid the sad fact that real people were dying, including babies who had gotten AIDS from their infected mothers. By the late 1980s the death toll was climbing toward a hundred thousand, and just about everyone in America knew someone whose life had been affected by the disease.

Bruce Woods Patterson, born in 1953, saw the devastating effect of AIDS on the gay community in New York City and pitched in to help.

GMHC [Gay Men's Health Crisis] had hired me on full time to work with Jerry Johnson on the AIDS hot line. What I didn't know at the time was that I had changed careers forever. We were all nonprofessionals back then, working by the seat of our pants and just trying to get GMHC's name out there. [Johnson's] instincts were what we call "client-centered" and "nondirective," which means that you accept the caller where they are, and you support them where they are, and you do not judge them, whatever you do. And you don't tell them what to do. You ask what they want to do and you ask them how they think they can do it, and in the end you help them figure out the options.

One of the great challenges of a hot line is that you get one chance to make a difference in the lives of the callers. In our case, we had to do that in under ten minutes, the prescribed time limit on most calls, and you have to maintain your anonymity, another requisite. It's really the only way to stay emotionally distant from the caller, although there are calls I carry around with me to this day. People called who were bed-bound, crying and sad with no hope. They'd start talking about how they used to be young and beautiful and had a future and how they had lost their identity, independence, and pride. A lot of people called and said, "I'm not afraid of death. It's getting there that scares me." Being stripped of all your dignity and losing half your body weight and having friends turn away just because they're in such pain they can't stand to see you that way is just horrible.

The level of ignorance and homophobia from some of the callers was just amazing. And the indifference was overwhelming. When I first started, prank callers would just say, "All you faggots should die!" *Click.* Thank you for sharing. It was bad enough all these people were dying and there was nothing that we could do about it, and then you've got people hating you for being sick or for helping sick people. Of course, you wanted badly to be able to say, "Where's your compassion? Who do you think you are? What's wrong with loving someone?"

My friends and I often talk about the community of infected and affected people. I am HIV-negative but have been affected deeply. We're all living with AIDS. I often wonder why I have been so lucky when so many of my friends and colleagues have died of AIDS. When I look back at the pictures of the early days at GMHC, it hits me every time that the majority of the people in them are no longer living. In the end, I have to be philosophical about it. I guess my job is to be there for everyone else. The best thing that I can do is just stay HIV-negative.

Throughout the 1980s, President Reagan maintained an iron-hard posture toward Communism. And this posture led to yet another government scandal. Nicaragua, a country in Central America, was led by a Communist government. Reagan wanted to help the "contra" rebels, who were fighting a guerrilla war against the government, but Congress had passed a law banning military aid to the contras. In a bizarre scheme to sidestep the law, American ammunition, spare parts for tanks, jet fighters, and missiles were sold to Iran to make money to fund the contra rebels.

Lieutenant Colonel Oliver North ran the secret

operation that eventually became known to the country as "Iran-contra." A decorated veteran of the Vietnam War, North was a patriot with an unshakable loyalty to the president. In testimony before Congress, North said that he believed he had acted "with authority from the president" in carrying out illegal operations in Central America and the Middle East. For America to be negotiating with the Ayatollah Khomeini's government was astonishing enough. But for illegal weapons sales to be linked to the White House was shocking. Just as they had during Watergate a decade earlier, Americans now asked, "What did the president know and when did he know it?" Iran-contra suggested one of two possibilities: Either the president himself was involved in an illegal international operation, or else he was a weak leader who did not know what was going on under his own nose. Neither possibility was flattering to the president who had promised a return to America's glory days.

As Americans faced their problems at home and abroad, it was comforting to know that at least the economy was still booming. That changed dramatically on October 19, 1987, Black Monday, when the stock market crashed. In one day the market lost 508 points, or 22.6 percent of its value—approximately $500 billion, an amount equivalent to the gross national product of France. Black

Monday reminded Americans of the stock market crash of 1929. But what really frightened them was the memory of what had followed—the miserable years of the Great Depression. For the next year, people watched and waited, but the depression never came. Slowly the market bounced back, and Americans breathed a sigh of relief.

In spite of—or perhaps because of—President Reagan's hard-line policy toward the Soviet Union and the renewed nuclear arms race, Communism was beginning to crack. In the late 1980s the Soviet Union was going through its most dramatic change since the 1917 revolution. Under the leadership of fifty-four-year-old Mikhail Gorbachev, who came to power in 1985, the Cold War began to thaw.

Even the crusty old members of the Politburo (the Soviet Congress) knew that their country had reached rock bottom. Industrial output was pitiful. Alcoholism was rampant. Workers were absent from their jobs much of the time. Housing shortages forced nearly a quarter of city residents to share bathrooms and kitchens. Food was scarce. Something drastic had to be done.

Gorbachev did not set out to bring an end to Communism in Russia. On the contrary, he saw himself as saving the Communist state. He started a three-part program to revitalize his ailing nation: *glasnost* (openness), *perestroika* (restructuring), and *demokratizatsiya* (democratization). And he presented this program not as a break with Soviet tradition, but as a way of reconnecting to the original principles of Lenin, the founder of the Soviet state.

It wasn't only in the Soviet Union that Communism was teetering. In Poland, a trade union called Solidarity had begun to challenge the Communist government in 1980. Although Solidarity had been shut down by the authorities in 1981, it still fought secretly for greater freedom in Poland. But in the late 1980s the world's attention was riveted on Mikhail Gorbachev. Within the Soviet Union itself, the excitement was building. Newspaper articles revealed corruption and mismanagement. Elections—real elections—were held. People began to talk openly about the past and the terrible things that had happened during Stalin's brutal regime. The truth about their own history had been forbidden to the Russian people. Gorbachev promised that there would be an end to secrecy and deception, the government's strongest weapons against its own people.

Marina Goldovskaya, born in 1941, is a filmmaker who took part in the new openness of the Gorbachev years.

In the mid-eighties I was working at the central television station in Moscow, making television programs on politics, on literature, art, social life, public affairs. This took half of my year, and the other half of the year I was a filmmaker for Ekram, a special film studio within the television station. All media in the USSR was heavily censored, and television was probably the most censored of them all. Everything we did was controlled by our administration. Every year we had to submit several proposals for the films for the next year. All of the proposals and concepts had to go through what was known as the "council of editors."

In early 1985 I submitted a proposal for a documentary film version of a book called *At My Mother's,* by Anatoly Streliany. He was a talented writer with independent ideas and a point of view that was not in line with the Communist Party. Because of his views he had a difficult time getting his works published. But this particular book was not overtly political. It described a visit he made to his mother's home in the village he grew up in, and it gave a very interesting portrait of the village. We got this proposal through all the censors, and it was put into the plan for 1986.

Even before we started working on *At My Mother's,* we got a sense that somehow things were changing. For a long time it had seemed as if something just had to change, because the whole country was stagnating. For so many years, the people who had ruled our country were old and outdated. We were so ashamed when we saw these old faces reading their speeches. They were not able to even read them properly, they were so old.

When Streliany and I started working on this film, I thought that we could take advantage of the changing atmosphere to do something more useful, more interesting. Something that could somehow help to push this process of change. So instead of making a documentary film based on his book, we decided to make a film about farmers and the struggle between the individual and the communal. We knew that our new idea would never be approved by the censors, but we decided to go ahead and make it anyway. We just acted as if we were still making a film based on our original approved proposal.

We traveled around talking to farmers and doing research, and we ended up in this little village called Ust-Vanga. And there I met this farmer named Nikolai Sivkov, who had been a member of the local collective farm but who had left in order to start his own little farm, belonging to him and his family. From the minute I met Sivkov, I understood that he would be a perfect character for a film. He was eloquent. He was witty. He was biting. In him, you could see all the controversy of our system. This man, who only had about two years of education, stood before the camera and talked about the advantages of private property and the inefficiencies of the collective, and how the Soviet farming system was preventing him from succeeding. The story of this man and his little farm was the perfect metaphor for the evils of the Soviet system. As I was shooting, I became so afraid. I understood that this could be the end of my career. The things that he was saying would never be shown on television. You just couldn't attack the collective like that. It was impossible. I was scared to death, but at the same time, I didn't have the strength to say to myself, no.

By the time I finished the film, which I called *Archamgelskiy Mujik,* which roughly translates to *A Real Peasant from Archamgelskiy,* Gorbachev had been in power for about a year, and he was such an inspiration for all of us. He was like fresh air. He was young, brave, and brighter than anybody else. It was something completely new to us; suddenly there was a lot of hope. We were all absolutely euphoric about Gorbachev. We thought that a new time was coming. Finally it seemed that people would stop telling lies. We were fed up with the lies we read in the newspaper. Everything we read was all fake, all lies. And everybody understood it, but nothing could be done. And suddenly there was somebody, Gorbachev.

When he started talking about *glasnost,* "openness," it was exciting. But change came very slowly at first, step by step. And while we were excited by everything, it was a very unsure time. Gorbachev still had a lot of opposition on the Politburo; there were still many of the old rulers around. So it was in this environment that we presented our film to a consultant from the Central Committee of the party. He was one of the members who was behind Gorbachev and who was ready for change, so he decided to take a chance and approve the broadcast of the film.

Archamgelskiy Mujik aired on a Thursday night. The next day the whole country was talking about it—in the buses, on the subway, in classrooms. I became famous in one minute. The television station wanted to repeat the film two weeks later, but suddenly there came an order to stop the broadcast. And the film was banned. Ultimately, because of the new policy of *glasnost,* they decided to air the film again. The fact that this film survived was a sure sign that Gorbachev was winning against the old guard. The feeling that we all had was that now we can start building a new life without lies and with good intentions. We felt that everything would go very quickly in the right direction,

> that the new life was very close. It took Gorbachev to make the first step, then everyone else just started to push the train.

In 1989 life in the Communist countries of Europe was transformed. No one, maybe not even Gorbachev himself, quite knew what he had started. Once reforms began, they took on a life of their own. When Gorbachev announced that the Soviet Union would no longer interfere with the governments of the eastern European countries, the threat of brute force that had kept the Communist regimes in power turned hollow. Poland, East Germany, Czechoslovakia, Bulgaria, Hungary, and Romania overthrew their Communist leaders. Even in China, students began protesting for democracy, although the Chinese government put down the uprising.

For Americans, it was amazing to watch Europe's post–World War II order fall before their eyes. And it wasn't the force of atomic bombs or the threats of a new tyrant that toppled these governments, but the power of an idea: liberty. Was it really possible that the Cold War was ending at last?

There were many heroes of the new times: Gorbachev, of course, and for many Reagan was a hero, too. For even though he was no longer president, many people believed it was Reagan's nuclear arms buildup that had forced Gorbachev to realize that Russia could not keep up and had to change. In

Poland, the head of the Solidarity union, Lech Walesa, had never given up the fight for freedom. And in Czechoslovakia, the writer Vaclav Havel had stood up to the Communist authorities, and had stood for justice and truth, since the Prague Spring of 1968.

The Iron Curtain that had divided Europe for so long was coming down. But the most dramatic event of this momentous era came in Berlin. Since 1961 the Berlin Wall had separated West Berlin from East Berlin, and many had died trying to cross it in desperate attempts to escape from East Germany. In 1989, with Communism vanishing like smoke around them, East Berliners marched to the wall shouting, "*Tor auf!* Open the gate!" The most hated symbol of Communism still separated Germans from each other. On the other side, West Berliners also crowded to the wall, wild with expectation.

Then, while guards put down their rifles, East Berliners climbed over the wall, jumping into the open arms of the West Berliners below. "The wall is gone, the wall is gone," people chanted happily. In a surge of joy, Berliners on both sides began pounding at it with hammers and chisels and pickaxes, turning the terrible wall into a pile of souvenir rocks. Everyone was giddy with excitement, with relief, with hope. The Cold War was over.

CHAPTER 4

Machine Dreams

1989–1999

In the final decade of the twentieth century the new, emerging world felt strangely different. The Cold War had defined so much of Western life for so long that it seemed as though a crippling lifelong pain had finally disappeared, and now it was time to learn how to walk all over again. But where, exactly, was the world headed?

In Europe the collapse of Communism was followed by puzzling questions. Could West Germany absorb East Germany and still remain stable? And if it did, would a unified Germany once again threaten world peace? In Eastern Europe the disappearance of powerful Communist governments brought age-old conflicts to the surface. Yugoslavia was split into warring ethnic groups. Czechoslovakia had broken apart into two states, the Czech Republic and Slovakia. And the Soviet Union had ceased to exist, bringing a handful of newly independent countries into the world. Would all these changes lead to more conflict?

Yet even as these changes shook Europe, there were many signs that democracy and capitalism were uniting the world. For the first time in fifty years the countries of eastern Europe were holding real elections. In places as far away as South Africa, democracy was triumphing. There black citizens were allowed to vote for the first time in 1994. They immediately elected as president Nelson Mandela, a man who had been in captivity for twenty-seven years for his pursuit of black equality.

Capitalism was taking hold in so many countries that a single enormous global marketplace was rapidly emerging. And this new capitalism had a distinctly American style, creating what one historian called "McWorld." As the Internet brought the world closer together, people wondered how this newly linked globe would coexist with the old hatreds that still pitted one ethnic group against another. Would the new technology—and the "global village" it was creating—be enough to bring a new age of world peace?

In the summer of 1990 a conflict erupted in the Persian Gulf that demonstrated what President George Bush called the "new world order." On

August 2 Iraq invaded the tiny country of Kuwait, which had large reserves of oil. The United Nations ordered Iraq's leader, Saddam Hussein, to withdraw his troops from Kuwait, but he steadfastly refused. By early 1991 more than two dozen allied nations gathered troops for an invasion of Iraq. Called "Desert Storm," the invasion was quickly successful. In just over forty days Iraq was driven out of Kuwait.

In a clear sign of the changing times, the Soviet Union joined the United States in its attack on Iraq. It was the first time since World War II that Americans and Soviets had fought on the same side. And the two nations fought together in a new role, as a kind of international police force countering acts of raw aggression. But just as important as the Gulf War's new alliance and new purpose was the way the war was fought. Both of the century's world wars had used increasingly destructive technology. Now, with satellites mapping the world and computer-guided bombs that could hit military targets with pinpoint precision, it seemed possible that war could become less destructive.

Mark Fox, born in 1956, led four major air wing strikes and flew eighteen combat missions during Desert Storm.

When I was a teenager, I really wanted to have a motorcycle, but my father was a doctor and he flatly refused. He said,

"I've pronounced too many kids your age dead. You can't have a motorcycle. But if you'd like to do something exciting, I'll help you learn how to fly." So I started flying gliders when I was in seventh grade. I had already known that I wanted to fly airplanes, even then. And when I discovered that there were airplanes that landed on ships, well, that sealed it for me. I entered the Naval Academy in 1974, the year after I graduated from high school.

In 1990 I was assigned to a squadron called VFA-81 in Air Wing 17, or the Sunliners, and we were attached to the USS *Saratoga*. We were scheduled to go in a normal deployment to the Middle East in August, so we were as trained and prepared as anybody when the Iraqis invaded Kuwait on August 2. We made it to the Red Sea, on the western side of the Saudi peninsula, by August 20 or 21. By that time Kuwait had been captured and there was this furious churn to get forces into the region to be able to deter any further aggression. We stayed there for five months before the war actually started. Now, I have a Christian faith, which helped me deal with the possibility of my own death. I felt that if the Lord called me home on this, then that's where I'd want to be. On the other hand, the idea of killing people was distasteful to me. Fortunately, with the technology and tactics at the time, we were far more precise about pinpointing the bad guys who were carrying weapons and driving tanks or airplanes. We could strike our targets with a minimal loss of life.

On January 15 we got word that the diplomatic efforts had failed and that we would soon initiate our opening sequence of strikes against Iraq. We had been training for these strikes for months, so there was a certain level of excitement—and a little bravado—at the anticipation of finally seeing action. At the same time, there was a lot of soul-searching and serious thought given to the fact that, no kidding, we're gonna do this. The opening strikes from the *Saratoga* were designed to suppress the defense around Baghdad. I wasn't on that first mission, but as I was being briefed for the second strike, we learned that one of our pilots was shot down and killed in the central part of Iraq. It was like ashes in our mouths. He was a good buddy of mine, a father of two— our children went to the same preschool together. It really helped bring home the realities of what we were doing.

My first combat mission was the first daylight strike on the seventeenth. From the Red Sea, over Saudi Arabia and into Iraq is somewhere between 650 and 750 nautical miles, one way. And there are no tactical airplanes that can go that distance without refueling, so on each mission we had to hook up with air force tanker planes. Typically there would be a sum total of maybe four or five air force tankers spaced out in a five-mile area in the sky, and there might be five navy airplanes attached to each tanker getting gas. So in that five-mile patch of sky there might be twenty-five to thirty navy jets all gassing up at the same time. It was an amazing sight, especially at night with all of the lights. It looked like the Empire State Building flying on its side through the sky.

We were about thirty miles south of the target and we were just now getting into the heart of the Iraqi surface-to-air missile envelopes. We got a radar lock on another group of airplanes flying very high and very slow just above our target, which is not where fighters defending a target would normally be. I wound up looking behind me for about the next minute, trying to see if this was a trap. These planes then turned and flew away from us. I had to decide whether to run these guys down or just go ahead and complete my mission. I thought to myself, "I came here to drop bombs, not to chase MIGs around." So I let him go and rolled in on the target. I dropped the bombs and did my jinks [erratic evasive maneuvers]. Now, I wasn't gonna come 640 nautical miles and not see my bombs hit their target, so I looked to see my four two-thousand-pound bombs falling together like four little fish in a pond. It was a really nice sight. But I could also see the muzzle flashes and the smoke and the dust coming from all over the field. There were literally dozens and dozens of little corkscrew bottle-rocket-looking things shooting up every which way down below me. It was clear that with all of this antiaircraft fire, it was no time for me to speculate anymore. So I went back into another series of adrenaline-fed jinks and peeked back at the target just in time to see my four bombs hit their target. And that was the first time I smiled all day. I turned back and headed for the carrier. Less than two hours after I landed, I was being briefed for my next mission.

Americans followed the progress of the Persian Gulf War on television, both on the three major networks and on the new Cable News Network. CNN offered Americans one of the most dramatic moments ever in television news, a chilling live picture of war as it happened. While the three networks had to decide whether to interrupt other programs to show the news, CNN was a twenty-four-hour window on the world. And CNN was not just broadcasting to American homes. By 1998 its cable links brought the news to 120 million homes overseas, making it the first truly global network. With so many people around the world watching the same images, it was hard not to feel that national boundaries were becoming less and less important.

In March 1991 American television screens were showing graphic footage of violence closer to home. In the early morning hours of March 3, a plumbing parts sales representative named George Holliday used his camcorder to capture the violent beating of Rodney King, a twenty-five-year-old black man, by four white Los Angeles police officers. The videotape was seen on television by millions of people.

Many black citizens asserted that the attack was not an isolated event. They said blacks were routinely treated with greater suspicion than whites and suffered harsher treatment from police officers. Now the whole world became an eyewitness to the kind of police brutality that African Americans claimed to face on a regular basis. It seemed unthinkable that the police officers arrested for the beating of Rodney King would not be convicted. Surely the videotape was proof of a serious crime. But the lawyers for the police officers argued that

King had been resisting arrest and was more threatening than the videotape made him look. The jury found the officers not guilty.

When the verdict was announced, Los Angeles erupted like a volcano. Hundreds of fires were set, and looters smashed into stores and ran off with millions of dollars' worth of merchandise. Innocent bystanders were attacked. In three days of unrest, fifty-four people were killed. It was the worst riot in America in this century.

Connie Chang, a daughter of Korean immigrants who was born in 1960, tried to help her parents protect their store from looters.

I had seen the Rodney King video on television and I did not agree with what the policemen did. I thought they were guilty of overreaction. And I believed that if he was a white guy instead of an African American, then they would not have done what they did to him. But I was not prepared for the riots. It was awful. Since the center of the rioting was in South-Central, I got worried because there are a lot of Korean businesses there, including my family's liquor store. My brother and an employee were in the store when the riots began, and my parents told them to shut the store down and come home.

In the first hours of the rioting, my

brother and I watched the coverage on TV and my parents listened to the Korean radio station. Because so many Korean shop owners were affected, Korean radio spent twenty-four hours a day doing nothing except coverage of the riots. Around seven-thirty my parents were listening when the station interviewed this one guy who started announcing the name of our store and saying that people were breaking the door in and taking some stuff out. So my parents went there and I joined them later.

Ours was a small store, a neighborhood store. And the majority of our clients were African American. We had black employees, too, and I treated them like, you know, my brother, and they treated me like their sister. But who starts looting our store? It's not neighborhood people. It's people coming from other areas. And they think it's all right because they don't know us and they think that all Koreans make money from out of their pockets.

When we got to the store, it looked terrible. An African American neighbor helped us get through the mess and into the store. Inside, we found that the lottery machine was gone. The telephones were gone. Even dishes and our rice cooker. The looters took a whole lot of merchandise and when they took it, you know, they dropped it, so the whole place smelled of alcohol. My two brothers and my cousin and my father all got up on the rooftop and stayed all night with guns, protecting the store. And they stayed on the rooftop I think three or four days. We were so worried about them we couldn't sleep. And yet even with my parents around, people were still trying to break the door down and get inside.

In the days after the riots, a lot of people came to the store and said they were sorry about the damages to our store. I think the damage was around $50,000 or $60,000 and insurance only paid half of that. Afterward my parents considered leaving America and going back to Korea. You know, it had hurt our feelings so much after the riot to see what it had done to our store. It's like all our hopes and dreams were gone. But if we went back to Korea, we would have to start all over again there, too.

After the riot I told everybody to put a smile on their face all the time. Just to show that we are human beings, too. When you are nice to people they won't be mean to you. They will be nice to you. Or at least we hope so.

———

In 1994 TV brought another dramatic trial into America's living rooms. O. J. Simpson, a well-known former football player who was now a sports commentator, movie actor, and advertising pitchman, was accused of the brutal murder of his ex-wife, Nicole, and her friend Ronald Goldman. Five days after the killings Americans flocked to their TVs to watch as Simpson fled from the police in a low-speed chase on a Los Angeles freeway. Simpson, in the backseat of a white Ford Bronco, gripped a revolver in one hand and a cellular phone in the other, announcing that he would kill himself if he couldn't see his mother.

By the time Simpson surrendered to the police, Americans were hooked on this tragic story. At first the case seemed to focus the nation's attention on the problem of domestic abuse. Simpson had been arrested before for hitting his wife, and she had once made a frightened 911 call when he had threatened her. But race soon became the dominant issue. Simpson was black, and his ex-wife and her friend were white. When it was discovered that one of the investigating officers had regularly used racist language, many African Americans became convinced that Simpson had been framed.

The trial was broadcast live on television for eight months and nine days. White Americans tended to believe that Simpson was guilty of two murders, while black Americans tended to believe he was the victim of a racist frame-up. It seemed as though the whole country was watching when, on October 3, 1995, the jury pronounced the verdict of not guilty. You could almost hear the nation split in two as most black Americans cheered and most whites shook their heads in disgust.

The dream of true integration, the kind that would fulfill America's promise of equality and unity, seemed more remote than ever. Two weeks after the Simpson verdict, Nation of Islam leader Louis Farrakhan led the Million Man March in Washington, D.C. Women and whites were excluded. By focusing only on black men, the march appeared to reject the ideal of integration that had inspired Martin Luther King Jr. when he led the famous March on Washington in 1963. The Million Man March did stress some positive values—respect for women, responsibility to families, and a condemnation of violence. Still, it seemed that King's vision of a tolerant, integrated America was now a part of history.

African American men around the nation, including T. Deon Warner, born in 1959, traveled to Washington for the Million Man March.

There is a perception in America that black males are the lowest, dirtiest, most conniving criminal people on this earth. Even black people think that. I know. I'm black and I am male and I have to overcome that image every day of my life. I am an attorney at a Houston law firm. And I'm a pretty good lawyer. I work on the forty-third floor of this modern sixty-four-story building. It's a class building, the kind of place where everybody wears suits every day. One day I was riding the elevator up to my floor when a white woman got on, and as soon as she saw me she started clutching her purse, as though to protect it from me. I thought, "This cannot be happening. Surely, I do not look as though I could ever be a threat to this woman or her purse." But, for some reason, to her I did.

So when they announced that there was going to be this Million Man March and that one of the goals of the march was to try to change the negative perception of the black male, I knew that I had to go. I didn't care how I got there or what I had to give up to go. It would be worth it to start changing the perception of black males. They were also trying to make a general statement that there are a lot of black males who don't go to prison, who are not beating their wives and girlfriends, and who are not out to rob everybody they see on the street.

I flew up from Houston and met a friend of mine from Michigan, and we made it down to the march site by about 4:45 A.M.

When we got to the grounds things were still pretty empty. And then I started seeing people coming out of the woodwork. I mean, they were coming from all directions. Just thousands and thousands of people. About an hour after I got there, there were people as far as I could see. I was surprised at how many men brought their sons with them. Young kids. I mean, they were ten, twelve, thirteen, fourteen. These men wanted their children to see this event, to be part of it.

There were many speakers throughout the day. And they came from different parts of the community: various religions, various backgrounds. One of the speakers was a twelve-year-old kid. And he gave a speech about how proud he was that he had a black father and that he was there at the march. He said that he represented the sons and daughters of each of the black males that were there. And then he made a demand of the audience. He asked that each person who was at that march go home and, if need be, rearrange their life so that they become a more positive role model in the communities. That they become better husbands to their wives. And a better father to their children. And then he asked everybody at the closing of the speech, "Will you do that for me?" Here's a twelve-year-old kid and in a very eloquent way he made a request that just seemed so simple and so basic and yet so compelling.

Black males have been painted as a subculture in our society. So the point about black pride and black male redemption is that we need to change our image. I don't think we need to change, necessarily, what we do. Because I think we do a pretty good job of being citizens in this community. I think we need to change the image of what people think we do. If we don't take charge to create and mold the perception that we want people to have of us, nobody else will. People need to understand that black males come in all different shapes and sizes just like white males or any other people in America. And if you can't generalize as to the other groups, the white males, the Asian males, et cetera, then you shouldn't generalize as to black males.

In the 1990s it seemed that much of the way life was conducted in the twentieth century was rapidly becoming "history." Technology accelerated the pace of change, rocketing America toward the twenty-first century. Old rules and traditions were out of date, and new ones were not quite established. A revolution was taking place. The Industrial

Revolution had brought in the machine age, which was coming to a close. The new revolution was ushering in the information age.

Computers had been around since the 1940s. The very name shows what they were expected to do—to compute, to add numbers. For decades these enormous machines could be found only in government offices and the headquarters of large corporations. What made the information age and the computer revolution possible was miniaturization. With the development of the microchip, the personal computer—a computer so small it could sit on a desk—became possible.

Almost overnight, computers changed play (video games), changed research (access to databases), and changed writing and editing (word processors). Computers even began to change work itself. With a modem, people could communicate through their office networks without leaving home. A scientist sitting in her pajamas in Minneapolis could argue with a colleague in Mozambique. More and more, the question about the computer wasn't "What can it do?" but "What can't it do?" Every day, it seemed, there was something new that this electronic wizard could do better or faster or more efficiently than people could.

By 1995 the computer was beginning to take people into the realm of science fiction—into cyberspace via the Internet. Originally developed by the Pentagon as a communications network that could withstand an atomic attack, the Internet was slow to catch on. But when it moved into mainstream American life, it swept in like a tidal wave. The most popular way to access the Internet was through the World Wide Web. Now people could find information, go shopping, or send electronic mail to the far corners of the world—all at the touch of a key.

Cyberspace pioneers ventured boldly into the virtual world online. Stacy Horn, born in 1956, was one of them.

When I was in my first semester at NYU, we had to call a place called the Well, and I was an instant addict. The Well is an online service based in California. It's a virtual community, where people get online to pretty much talk about anything under the sun. When I was in my last year of graduate school, I logged into the Well and someone said to me, "Hey, we heard that you were going to start the East Coast version of the Well." I had never said that, but all of a sudden it was like, "Duh, of course I can do that." So I just typed in, "Yes, I am."

In March 1990 Echo opened to the public. I came up with the name Echo because I had some vague idea like you throw your words out into the world and words come back. I couldn't get any investors interested because in 1989 nobody would believe me that the Internet was going to be hot.

I structured Echo so it was made up of different areas—we call them conferences. There's a books conference, a movies conference, an art conference, a New York conference, and within these conferences are conversations that fit under that general heading. The conversations are in what's called non-real time. So I can go into, say, the books conference and type in whatever I have to say. Then you can log in tomorrow, see what I've written, and add whatever you want to say about the subject. So the conversation keeps going on, and you can talk to these people regardless of who's logged in when. It's actually better than a live conversation. In a conversation that's non-real time, you can take your time and really consider your thoughts and say something more substantial.

On the Internet, you get to know someone from the inside out first, whereas in the physical world it's from the outside in. Each way has its pluses and minuses. People are people, and they're no different online than they are anywhere else. We don't sit down at our computers and all of a sudden become unreal. If I say "I love you" to someone on the phone, does that make it not real? So if I say it on a computer, why would that make it not real?

The Internet played a big part in making the world seem smaller. People could now communicate with each other around the world, instantly, without laws or controls or many government restrictions. Many believed that the computer and the fax machine were vital to the collapse of Communism. A system that depended on controlling information simply could not withstand the new technologies. All people needed for ideas and information to flow was a computer and a phone line.

Still, while enthusiasm for the World Wide Web raced around the globe, there was also skepticism. Some intellectuals worried about its impact on society. With technology dominating our lives, would we become slaves to the machines? Would the creation of so many virtual worlds make people care less about the real world?

Mistrust of technology inspired the "Unabomber." Theodore Kaczynski, a Harvard-educated hermit, had systematically targeted people in the technology industry. His mail bombs killed three people and injured twenty-three in sixteen separate attacks. They were an insane attempt to slow the progress of science and technology.

But Kaczynski's bombs were not as deadly as the work of Timothy McVeigh. On April 19, 1995, a truck bomb exploded outside a federal building in Oklahoma City, collapsing its nine floors. For days rescue workers pawed through the wreckage looking for survivors as outrage and despair gripped the nation. In the end, 168 people were dead, including 19 children who were in the building's day-care center.

How could there be a terrorist bombing in the heartland of the country? At first wild racist rumors placed the blame on "Middle Eastern types." But as federal agents began to investigate, a more disturbing theory arose. April 19 was a date well known to the FBI and other law enforcement agencies of the federal government. Two years previously on that date, the standoff at the Branch Davidian compound in Waco, Texas, had ended in a deadly fire. The Branch Davidians were a religious cult whose members had stockpiled weapons and were resisting investigation by federal authorities into how their children were being treated. On April 19, 1993, a total of eighty-four people died when federal agents attacked the compound.

For those on the political far right, Waco became a symbol of the tyranny of the federal government. The bombing of the federal building in Oklahoma City on April 19 was an act of revenge carried out not by foreign terrorists, but by an American veteran of the Persian Gulf War.

The approaching millennium seemed to focus attention on chaos, destruction, and death. Increasingly the evening news mentioned Dr. Jack Kevorkian, the Michigan physician known as "Dr.

Death," who assisted terminally ill people to commit suicide. For decades medical advances had focused on prolonging life even through terrible disease. Medicine seemed unwilling to let the dying die. But by the nineties the "right-to-die" movement was gaining momentum. Advocates of the "right to die" suggested that there were greater concerns for patients and their families than simply being kept alive by machines regardless of the quality of life. The "right to die" with peace and dignity was seen as a humane concern that medical technology was ignoring.

Opponents of the "right to die" argued that doctors would soon be deciding who lived and who died, giving people a power that rightfully belonged to nature or to God. It was an argument that pitted the control of the individual against the power of fate, the quality of life against the sanctity of life. But while the controversy raged, real people still had to cope with agonizing decisions.

Christina Walker Campi, born in 1951, struggled with the best way to care for her dying husband.

In 1996 my husband, Tom, became sick with what we thought was bronchitis. After antibiotics failed, he went through a battery of tests: chest X rays, MRI, CAT scan, bone scan, liver biopsy, ultrasound. It was like Western medicine at its best and its worst. At the end of it all they diagnosed him with metastasized lung cancer. And what was worse was that it had spread to his trachea and his liver. The next day I got our oncologist [cancer specialist] alone. He said, "What do you want to know?" I said, "I want to know how long he has." He said, "Six to nine months." My knees buckled.

For the next several months Tom went through round after round of chemotherapy and treatments, but his cancer continued to spread. The day that I decided to stop treatment on Tom, his most recent MRI showed that the cancer had moved to his brain. He had already started to show some neurological symptoms. He still knew who I was, but he was confused in his thinking. Tom was a brilliant guy who loved to talk, and to see him starting to get confused and losing control of himself was awful. He felt so humiliated. And he was in terrible pain. The cancer had also moved into his bones, which is the most painful cancer of all. I decided to ease his pain with morphine, knowing that this would hasten his death. I knew what I was doing. I was pretty clearheaded at that point. But I'm still tortured by the possibility that he could have had just a short amount of time more, a couple more days. I feel horrible that I was the one with sole control over this decision.

After Tom and I signed the DNR [do not resuscitate] order, he was moved to a private room and he was put on a morphine drip. After he was on the morphine for a while, a friend of mine, who happened to be a doctor on staff at the hospital, came by and said, "You know, he's not going to last more than a couple of hours right now." And I started to cry, because his children were on their way in from California to say good-bye, and I was afraid he would die before they got there. My friend told me to have them turn the morphine pump off, and then he'd come out of it for a little while. He woke up the next morning, and he saw his kids, and he kissed them, he hugged them. He kind of squeezed my hand a little bit, and he went back to sleep. And that was it; he never woke up again. Luckily, because I had them decrease the dosage, he was able to hold on to see his kids. But I had no guidance, no help on this at all except that I happened to have this friend who's on staff there. He would've died that night and not seen his kids had we not turned the morphine pump off.

We had been helped by the doctors with all sorts of treatment, but their help pretty much stopped when the treatment stopped. These were good doctors, with whom my husband was very attached, but they were trained to prolong life, not to deal with the dying process. I was left with this enormous feeling of having been abandoned.

This experience made me realize that birth and death are equally important, but we only pay attention to the birth end of it. Whenever you read anything about death or dying, you inevitably read about Dr. Kevorkian and about physician-assisted suicide. That is just a red herring in the whole discussion of death and dying. It has little to do with ordinary illness and dying. Death is like our dirty little secret. We all come to this world, but we pretend we are all not going to go out of it.

I think Americans especially are terrified of death. We're a can-do population, so death seems like a terrible failure to us. We assign blame rather than see death for what it is, which is the way it's going to end for all of us.

When England's Princess Diana died in a car crash in 1997, the new communications technology spread the news across the globe instantly. Although she and Prince Charles were divorced and Diana never would have been queen, she was known everywhere, and her death caused an enormous outpouring of grief. On the day of her funeral, more than a million people lined the streets of London to watch the coffin pass by. Billions more watched on television. Why did so many people mourn her passing? Diana was beautiful and charming, and she had supported many charities. But her connection to people seemed to go deeper than her outward accomplishments. People felt more loyalty to her than to the royal family she had married into. She was the "people's princess," and the sad story of youth and beauty and promise so tragically cut short moved people around the world to tears.

The funeral of Princess Diana could be seen as a bookend for the century, matching the grand funeral of England's Queen Victoria in 1901, which marked the passing of the 1800s. Life has changed more in the hundred years since Queen Victoria's death than it did in the thousand years that went before. And most of the changes the twentieth century brought were for the better. Think about this: The life expectancy of an American born in 1905 was only forty-nine years; by 1998 it was seventy-six years. Think, too, about the fact that in the late 1800s every other death was that of a baby. And remember how many people at the beginning of the century lived not only without electricity or telephones or TVs or computers, but also without the basic freedoms that democracy now gives them.

It is true that the world completely failed to realize the fantasies of a golden age that many people dreamed of at the start of the twentieth century. Even the sophisticated streets of the new "global community" are still the scene of violence and bloodshed. In the twentieth century people believed that human will could control the forces of existence through science and technology. Yet at the end of the century a new humility seemed to be growing, a sense that there are limits to what people can control.

There is still no communications tool more powerful than the family story, and the family stories handed down from this century have all too often been tales of oppression, of prejudice, of war, of sorrow. In every family's history are ancestors who survived the terror of World War I, the horrors of the Holocaust, the injustices of the Jim Crow laws, or the grim grip of Communism. Both politics and technology made the twentieth century a century of killing. But politics and technology also provide us with hope for the future. And it is hope that carries us forward into the unknown territory we will explore in the next century.

INDEX

Read more about our nation's history
in these companion volumes. . . .

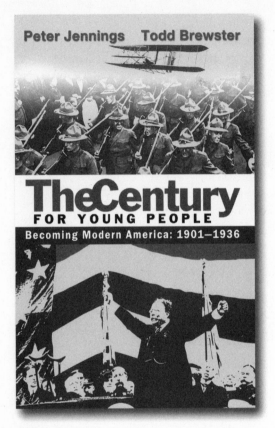

Peter Jennings   Todd Brewster

TheCentury
FOR YOUNG PEOPLE
Becoming Modern America: 1901–1936

The Century

for Young People

Becoming Modern America
1901–1936

Imagine . . .
watching the Wright brothers rise into the sky,
demonstrating for women's right to vote,
fighting in the trenches during World War I,
hearing the first voice crackle over the radio,
riding the rails as a hobo during the Great Depression.

Let your imagination soar as you experience all the
drama of the twentieth century through the eyes of the
people who lived it. The vivid stories of the
eyewitnesses at the center of this narrative bring to life
the most inspiring, surprising, and terrifying events of
the past hundred years. These are the voices of the
ordinary people—woman and men, children and
adults—who were a part of history in the making. Their
joys and sorrows, hopes and fears provide a compelling
insider's look at the momentous events that have
reshaped the world and transformed the everyday lives
of all of us in a century of incredible changes.

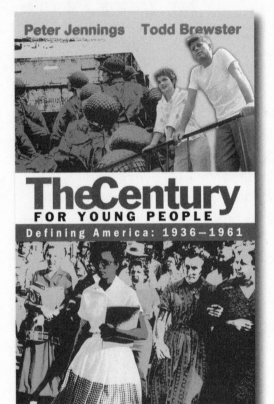

Peter Jennings   Todd Brewster

TheCentury
FOR YOUNG PEOPLE

Defining America: 1936—1961

The Century
for Young People

Defining America
1936–1961

Imagine . . .
landing in a hail of bullets on a Normandy beach,
being blacklisted as a Communist and pressured to
betray your friends and coworkers,
watching the first images spring to life on television,
walking eight miles in the rain to demand equal rights.

Let your imagination soar as you experience all the
drama of the twentieth century through the eyes of the
people who lived it. The vivid stories of the
eyewitnesses at the center of this narrative bring to life
the most inspiring, surprising, and terrifying events of
the past hundred years. These are the voices of the
ordinary people—woman and men, children and
adults—who were a part of history in the making. Their
joys and sorrows, hopes and fears provide a compelling
insider's look at the momentous events that have
reshaped the world and transformed the everyday lives
of all of us in a century of incredible changes.